The Complete Guide to

Ragdoll Cats

Tarah Schwartz

Publication Data

Tarah Schwartz
The Complete Guide to Ragdoll Cats – First edition.
Summary: "Successfully raising a Ragdoll cat from kitty to old age"
Provided by publisher.
ISBN: 978-1-954288-83-6
[1. The Complete Guide to Ragdoll Cats – Non-Fiction] I. Title.

Design by Sorin Rădulescu
First paperback edition, 2023

TABLE OF CONTENTS

Chapter 5

Chapter 6

Chapter 7

CHAPTER 1

Ragdoll Cats – A Unique and Wonderful Breed

Physical Characteristics

Ragdolls are well-balanced cats with an overall appearance of grace and power. They are one of the largest breeds of cats, with males weighing as much as 20 pounds. Females are slightly smaller, typically between 10 to 20 pounds. The Ragdoll's head is large and wedge-shaped with medium-sized, wide-set ears. The eyes are large and always blue. Ragdolls have a long, rectangular bodies with heavy boning. Their legs are moderately long, with the hind legs slightly longer than the front. The paws are proportionately large and tufted. The Ragdoll's tail should be long with a full plume of fur.

The Ragdoll's coat is one of the breed's signature characteristics. They are semi-longhaired with abundant guard hairs and a minimal woolly undercoat. The silky coat comes in four color patterns: colorpoint, mitted, bi-color, and van. The colorpoint coat is generally pale, with darker-colored ears, paws, face, and tail. A mitted coat is similar to a colorpoint but with white markings on all four feet. There may also be a white blaze, star, or hourglass on the forehead and nose. Bi-color Ragdolls have the same dark shading on the ears, face, and tail but with the addition of white on the face, chin, neck, and underside. The feet and legs should also be white. Van Ragdolls have dark points on the ears, face, and tail, with a glistening white coat covering the body, legs, and paws. The points of any coat pattern may be one of six colors: seal, blue, chocolate, lilac,

Photo Courtesy of
Stormi Nell - FamilytimeRags

red, and cream. Additionally, the points may be solid-colored, lynx, or tortie. Regardless of color and coat pattern, most Ragdolls tend to darken with age.

Temperament and Behavior

Ragdolls are a very social breed. They want to be with you, and they want to be doing whatever you're doing. If you are at your desk, they will probably be on your desk. If you are heading to the bathroom, you'll probably have a friend following right behind you.

STORMI NELL
Familytime Rags

HELPFUL TIP

Ragdoll Fanciers' Club (RFC)

The Ragdoll Fanciers' Club (RFC) is the Cat Fanciers' Federation's (CFF) official Ragdoll Breed Club in the United States. This club began as the Ragdoll Society in February 1975 and was founded by Denny and Laura Dayton. In 1976, the Ragdoll Society was incorporated with CFF and became the Ragdoll Fanciers' Club in May 1978. The primary objective of this club is to preserve the Ragdoll breed. For more information about the RFC, visit www. ragdollfanciersclub.org.

Ragdolls are famous for their outgoing, friendly personalities. They are more human-oriented than many breeds and will happily greet you at the door and follow you around your home. Ragdolls are gentle cats that typically love affection and attention from their favorite person or people. Many are accepting of strangers, but some Ragdolls may be a bit standoffish with unfamiliar people.

In general, Ragdolls are not big jumpers or climbers and usually prefer to spend more time on the floor than on elevated surfaces. They do not usually play rough, instead preferring to play without extending their claws. Ragdolls are known for their "dog-like" personalities and are typically easy to train and eager to engage in play. Since Ragdolls are generally well-behaved and easy to care for, they make great companions for families and individuals of all ages, including seniors and cat-savvy children. Ragdolls are also an intelligent breed, which aids in training. They are very observant and pick up the rules of the household quickly.

Reaching Full Maturity

Ragdoll kittens are born at an average weight of around three ounces. The kittens grow quickly and generally open their eyes at around two weeks of age, though they cannot see clearly until about three weeks of age. At four weeks of age, the kittens can usually move around well and begin to clean themselves. After five weeks, Ragdoll kittens grow rapidly, and with their increased level of activity, they will also begin to eat more. At this age, most breeders begin to supplement the mother's milk with wet and dry food. Kittens are typically weaned off their mother's milk between eight and 10 weeks of age.

Between three and six months, Ragdoll kittens experience a rapid period of growth. By five months, most Ragdoll kittens weigh at least four pounds and will continue to gain around a pound per month until around a year of age. During this period of rapid growth, there may be times when a kitten's body proportions are a little unusual. Their heavy bone structure may cause a kitten's hind legs to appear longer than normal, but with time they will grow into the proper proportions. At around four or five months, kittens will also begin to lose their baby teeth and replace them with adult teeth.

Ragdolls reach their teenage to young adult stage between six and 12 months. Their growth tends to slow a bit during this period, so it may be necessary to reduce food intake. Some kittens may begin to develop a fuller coat or mane during this period, but others may take longer. Ragdoll kittens reach sexual maturity between seven and nine months. By a year old, Ragdolls will more or less look like adult cats, and growth will slow but not stop.

Since Ragdolls are a large breed, they tend to take longer to fully mature than some smaller breeds of cats. This breed typically doesn't

*Photo Courtesy of
Melissa Firestone - Rockstar Ragdolls*

develop its full coat color until around two years of age. The cats will continue to grow slowly beyond that, reaching their full adult size and weight around four years.

Is a Ragdoll Cat Right for You?

> 66
>
> *The best kind of home for a Ragdoll is a family that will understand the needs of a Ragdoll. Ragdolls are dependent and not independent like some breeds are. They want to be around your family members and expect to hang around you while you're watching TV, reading, or working from home. They may be in your lap, or, yes, if you're working, they could be on your keyboard! A family has to know that a Ragdoll wants to be PART of your day-to-day life.*
>
> MELISSA FIRESTONE
> *Rockstar Ragdolls*
>
> 99

Ragdolls are a stunning breed, and many people immediately fall in love with their size and unique appearance. However, they are not the ideal cat for everyone, so it's important to consider whether they are a good match for you and your lifestyle before bringing one home. Cats are

Photo Courtesy of Bette Willette

a huge responsibility, so it's crucial to really consider this decision.

Ragdolls are known for their friendly, outgoing personalities, but they can be somewhat demanding at times. They crave attention from their owners, so if you aren't fond of having your cat follow you around the house like a shadow, you may need to consider a different breed. This is not a breed that you can leave alone for long periods of time each day. Ragdolls need regular attention and affection.

Photo Courtesy of Angie Winstead

CATS WELCOME
(PEOPLE TOLERATED)

It's also important to remember that all cats are individuals, and Ragdolls are no different. Some Ragdolls may be less affectionate or even skittish. Buying from a reputable breeder can help ensure your new cat meets your expectations, but there are never guarantees. Knowing what type of personality will work best for your family will help you to find your ideal cat.

Though the Ragdoll's coat is one of its most beautiful characteristics, they are not a low-maintenance breed in terms of grooming. Their silky coats can become matted if neglected, so you need to be prepared to brush your cat on a regular basis. If you choose not to groom your Ragdoll yourself, you'll need to make sure you find a professional cat groomer within your budget. Regular grooming can also help reduce the amount of hair left around your home. However, no matter how much you brush your cat, Ragdolls do shed, so be prepared for regular vacuuming. The breed's signature coat can also cause issues for people with allergies, so it's important to be aware of whether you may have a reaction before bringing a kitten home.

Speaking of budget, caring for any cat can be expensive, but a purebred cat will be even more costly. The price you'll pay for a well-bred Ragdoll will depend on the area you live in, but most are not cheap. After you bring home your Ragdoll, you'll also need to make sure you can afford the essentials, including food, beds, scratching posts, and more. Routine and emergency vet care can also be expensive, so you'll need to be prepared for the costs associated with maintaining your Ragdoll's health.

Ragdolls are fun, friendly, beautiful cats, but they can be a lot of work. Bringing a Ragdoll cat into your home should not be an impulsive decision. It's also important to make sure that everyone in your household is on the same page. After thoroughly considering your options, you can then decide whether a Ragdoll is right for you and your family.

CHAPTER 2

History of the Ragdoll Cat

The Origins of the Ragdoll

The Ragdoll cat was originally developed in the 1960s by Ann Baker, a cat breeder in Riverside, California. The breed began with a white, longhaired female cat named Josephine. Josephine was originally found wandering throughout Baker's neighborhood and was bred to other cats owned or found by Baker.

All of Josephine's offspring had particularly endearing temperaments, so Baker decided to start a breeding program that would eventually result in the Ragdoll breed. There are various accounts of which cats were used in the development of the Ragdoll, but none are able to be verified. It's believed that Josephine was bred to one of the cats that Baker had borrowed for her black Persian breeding program, but there is no record of the males bred to Josephine in the beginning. Regardless of how it all began, the result was the large, floppy, lovable cat known today as the Ragdoll.

In addition to Josephine, Baker also obtained one of her sons, a black kitten named Blackie. Shortly thereafter, it was discovered that Blackie had a half-brother, who is said to have resembled a Birman cat. Baker named that cat Raggedy Ann Daddy Warbucks. Even Baker herself was not certain who Daddy Warbucks' sire was, so it's difficult to discuss the first few generations of the program with any certainty. Both Blackie and Daddy Warbucks became essential additions to the breeding program. Josephine was eventually bred to both Blackie and Daddy Warbucks to produce the foundations of the Ragdoll breed.

Photo Courtesy of
Amanda Carter

Unfortunately, Ann Baker was unable to use any more of Josephine's offspring in her breeding program after a tragic incident. Josephine began getting into fights with the family dog, and Baker's husband eventually took Josephine and her litter at the time to be destroyed. Following this tragedy, Baker was left with three essential cats: Daddy Warbucks, Buckwheat (a daughter of Josephine and Blackie), and Fugianna (a daughter of Josephine and Daddy Warbucks). The offspring of these cats were eventually divided into two categories: the Light Side and the Dark Side. Fugianna, who was lighter colored, would go on to produce the Light Side lineage, while Buckwheat, a black cat, would found the Dark Side.

Ragdoll Myths and Truths

There are a number of mysteries surrounding the Ragdoll breed's origins and signature characteristics. One account claims that Josephine was hit by a car and left immune to pain, resulting in a floppy demeanor when handled. Before her accident, her kittens were supposedly like every other cat, but afterward, it's said that they, too, gained her new-found relaxed and friendly character. Baker has often been credited with the unusual stories surrounding the Ragdoll's origins. Unfortunately, little information can be accurately verified, as Baker herself was the only available source at the time. Despite the number of mysteries and false-hoods surrounding the breed, one true fact is that all legitimate Ragdoll cats can be traced back to Josephine.

More verifiable information became available after Baker eventually got her new breed registered with the National Cat Fanciers Association. At that time, it was Baker's firm belief that her strict and unusual breeding policy was the only way to produce true Ragdoll cats. Her plan required that the cats had to be line bred for seven generations, never using male offspring, but rather a male named who was purchased specifically for the program. After the seventh generation, the female offspring could then be bred to another direct son of Josephine. Baker eventually enlisted the help of a few breeders contracted as franchises to continue her breeding program under her strict guidance.

HISTORICAL FACT
Groovy Kittens

Now one of America's most popular longhaired breeds, Ragdoll cats have somewhat unconventional origins. The world can thank a breeder named Ann Baker, who bred semi-feral cats from a friend's farm to eventually produce what we know as the Ragdoll breed. Baker began selling these cats in the late 1960s.

The Ragdoll's history took an interesting turn in 1969 when Baker sold a breeding pair of Ragdolls to the Dayton family, who owned Blossom Time Cattery. The Daytons did not have any initial agreements in place with Baker but planned to use that initial breeding pair to continue refining the Ragdoll breed. Baker then surprised the couple when she attempted to implement a franchise

Photo Courtesy of Susan L Anderson

agreement and demanded a large sum of money in exchange. When the Daytons refused to pay, Baker attempted to bring a lawsuit against the couple but was unsuccessful. The Daytons were eventually able to file a restraining order against Baker to prevent the alleged harassment and slander they were being subjected to. Despite the legal challenges, they continued their breeding program and were eventually able to produce

Photo Courtesy of
Julie Stocker

Ragdolls featuring the breed's now signature characteristics, including icy blue eyes and the four recognized coat patterns of the modern Ragdoll.

Even though the Ragdoll was now being further developed by another cattery, Ann Baker did her best to maintain control over the breed. In 1971, Baker founded the International Ragdoll Cat Association (IRCA), which strictly dictated how the Ragdoll could be bred. In response, the Dayton family founded the Ragdoll Fanciers Club International (RFCI) to further promote the breed in their own way. Despite Baker's attempts to control the Ragdoll breed, the Daytons were more successful in their development and promotion. Undoubtedly, the breed would not be where it is today if it had not been for them.

A few of Ann Baker's cats were also purchased by Curt Gehm. The cats purchased by Gehm were mink, solid, and sepia-colored Ragdolls, which were not acceptable colors for the Daytons' breeding program. Gehm began outcrossing those cats to other breeds to eventually produce a new breed called the Ragamuffin. Ragamuffins shared a few traits with the original Ragdoll, including the tendency to go limp when picked up, but they quickly became a distinctly different breed.

The Modern Ragdoll Cat

Today, the Ragdoll cat has been formally recognized by major cat registries, including the Cat Fanciers' Association (CFA) and I he International Cat Association (TICA). Thanks to its stunning appearance and laid-back personality, the Ragdoll has become one of the most popular breeds of cats worldwide. According to the CFA's registrations statistics, the Ragdoll was the most popular purebred cat from 2019 to 2021. According to the Governing Council of the Cat Fancy (GCCF) in the UK, the Ragdoll is ranked overall as the second most popular breed, only being beaten by the British Shorthair.

Though there has been some debate over solid, mink, and sepia-colored Ragdolls, they are now allowed to be shown at all TICA-sanctioned shows under the "New Traits" category. Previously, they were not considered true Ragdolls and were unable to be shown. This is because many of these cats were produced using unauthorized outcrosses to other breeds, such as Maine Coons and Persians. Dedicated Ragdoll breeders are currently working toward getting these "nontraditional" coat colors officially recognized, but they must follow a stringent process in order to be accepted in the championship class alongside traditional Ragdolls.

Photo Courtesy of Stephanie Wineland

CHAPTER 3

Purchasing a Ragdoll Cat

Buying vs. Adopting

O nce you've decided that a Ragdoll is the right cat for you and your lifestyle, it's time to decide whether you would prefer to buy from a breeder or adopt from a shelter or rescue organization. There are pros and cons to both options, so it's important to consider your goals and expectations before making a decision. You will also want to

Photo Courtesy of
Melissa Firestone - Rockstar Ragdolls

consider whether you're interested in a kitten or an adult cat.

Kittens are typically more work than adult cats and require more socialization and veterinary care during the first year. For busy households, an adult cat may provide the desired companionship but without the extra work. However, the charm of a Ragdoll kitten is undeniable, and many people enjoy raising their Ragdolls from a young age despite the effort. Kittens tend to get adopted quicker, but there are often many lovely adult cats looking for a good home. You should

HELPFUL TIP

Ragdoll Fanciers' Club International (RFCI)

Many potential Ragdoll owners turn to a cat association when seeking a responsible breeder. The RFC is an excellent resource for prospective Ragdoll owners in the United States, but what about elsewhere? The Ragdoll Fanciers' Club International (RFCI), founded in 1975, maintains a compendium of registered international breeders who have signed a code of conduct to qualify for RFCI membership. For more information about this club, visit www.rfci.org.

also consider any pets you already have at home. A rambunctious kitten may be too much for an elderly cat, whereas an adult cat would have a more appropriate energy level. Likewise, if you already have an active pet at home, a spunky kitten may be an ideal companion.

If you are interested in showing your cat or eventually getting into breeding, your best option is to work with a reputable Ragdoll breeder. It will be impossible for you to find a show- or breeding-quality Ragdoll at a shelter. A reputable breeder will be able to match you to the right cat for your lifestyle and goals. However, it's important to understand that this is not the cheapest option. Purebred Ragdoll cats are not inexpensive, especially if you intend to find one of exceptional quality. More information on how to find a reputable Ragdoll breeder will be covered in the next chapter.

If you are only interested in bringing home a new companion, you will have the option to get your cat from either a breeder or a rescue. Both choices have their own benefits, so you will need to weigh your options. Many breeders provide kitten owners with a lifetime of support, as well as a safety net for the kitten if they are no longer able to provide a home.

Photo Courtesy of
Mindy Ferreira - Bellapalazzo Ragdolls

However, it can be more expensive to purchase from a breeder, and you may be paying upward of $1,000 for your new Ragdoll. If the breeder has any adult cats looking for a new home, they may be less expensive than a kitten. Adopting a cat from a shelter can be much cheaper, but it may be a challenge to find a purebred Ragdoll in a rescue.

Ragdolls from a rescue are often already spayed or neutered and up-to-date on vaccines. If you buy a cat from a breeder, you may be responsible for some or all of these initial costs in addition to the purchase price. However, a Ragdoll from a reputable breeder will likely come with a health guarantee, hopefully saving you money on vet bills in the long run.

It's important to note that whether you choose to buy your Ragdoll from a breeder or a rescue, you should be prepared for a wait. Ragdolls are in high demand, and ethical breeders often have waitlists for their litters. If you choose to work with a rescue, you may also find yourself waiting to be approved for adoption and waiting for the perfect cat to arrive at the shelter. It can be tempting to skip the wait and buy a kitten from a backyard breeder, but a quality Ragdoll is worth the wait. It's much better to delay your adoption plans by a few months than support the unethical breeding of animals.

Backyard breeders and pet stores may have Ragdoll kittens on demand, but purchasing from these places should be discouraged. They are not producing kittens for the betterment of the breed but instead to increase their bank account balance. Backyard breeders and kitten mills do not health test their cats prior to breeding and often produce unhealthy kittens as a result. They are not bred for good temperaments, and the kittens may not behave like typical Ragdolls. Since the cats are not bred to conform to the breed standard, they may not look like Ragdolls once they reach maturity. It's far better to work with reputable people who care about the health and well-being of their cats and the Ragdoll breed as a whole. It may take longer to connect with your dream cat, but you will be much happier with your new Ragdoll knowing you are supporting ethical breeders and rescue organizations instead of greedy backyard breeders or kitten mills.

Rescues and Shelters

As with breeders, it's important to make sure you adopt from a reputable rescue organization. Not all organizations operate with the animals' best interests in mind, so you need to be prepared to do your research. Some rescues may label cats as Ragdolls because they look somewhat similar, but you will not be bringing home a cat with the famous Ragdoll temperament. The reputation of a rescue organization can often be discovered with a quick internet search. Bad reviews on social media are also a red flag, so be sure to look up an organization before contacting them about adoption.

If you are interested in adopting a Ragdoll cat, it's recommended to search for a breed-specific rescue organization. Since the Ragdoll is a popular breed, there are a number of rescues across the United States that specialize in connecting Ragdolls of all ages with their new owners. These organizations are familiar with the breed, so they will often be able to tell a purebred Ragdoll from a lookalike. They will also be able to work with you to ensure that you bring home a cat that best matches your lifestyle.

Since Ragdolls are a popular breed, it's important to realize that they are in high demand. Even if a rescue does not have your ideal cat, it's often worth submitting an application so that you can be approved once your dream cat arrives at the rescue. Otherwise, the cat may find a new home while you're still waiting for your adoption application to be approved. Remember, rescue organizations are generally run by volunteers. It can sometimes be difficult to thoroughly screen potential adopters in a timely manner.

If you live in a rural area, it may be difficult to find a rescue nearby. Most rescues will require you to pick up the cat in person, so be prepared to travel if necessary. However, some rescues may have rules about adopting to out-of-state homes, so be sure to talk to a rescue representative before making the trip. Many rescues also work with other organizations to arrange the transport of the animals in their care to their forever homes, so you may want to ask about this possibility if your ideal Ragdoll is far away.

The cost to adopt a Ragdoll through a rescue organization will be less than buying from a breeder, but many rescues charge more for purebred cats. You can expect to pay an adoption fee between $100–$300 on average. Additionally, you can expect to pay more for kittens

*Photo Courtesy of
Christine Hillis*

than adult cats. Many rescues have reduced adoption fees on older cats to encourage people to adopt seniors that may otherwise be overlooked.

Photo Courtesy of Vickie Hatfield

Tips for Adoption

Just as you would when choosing a cat from a breeder, it's important not to prioritize the appearance of your new Ragdoll over the temperament. Ragdolls are beautiful cats and can be easy to fall in love with at first sight, but you should get to know the cat to make sure that it will fit into your current lifestyle.

You can start by asking shelter staff or foster volunteers about the Ragdoll you're interested in, especially if the cat has been with the organization for some time. They may be able to provide you with more information about the cat's personality and habits. It's not uncommon for cats in a rescue to be nervous around new people, so the cat may behave differently around familiar faces. It's important to ask questions about the cat's preferences as well. Some cats may prefer a quiet household, while others don't mind a house full of children and other pets.

You may want to ask questions about the following:
- Eating habits
- Food preferences
- Behavior toward other cats
- Behavior toward children
- Behavior toward dogs or other pets
- Litter box habits
- Play habits
- Activity level
- How vocal the cat may be

Photo Courtesy of Ebah Wolf

- Any bad habits the cat may have
- Overall health
- Vaccination status
- Whether the cat has been spayed or neutered

It can be helpful to be flexible in what you're looking for in a Ragdoll. If you've set out to adopt a kitten, you may want to expand your search to include adult cats as well. It's fine to have a preference in terms of coat color, but you may also want to consider cats of other colors too. The same applies to gender preferences. You just might find the perfect feline friend, even if he or she isn't exactly what you were looking for. If you are interested in a cat, but one doesn't check all your boxes, consider spending some time together anyway. You may be surprised by a special connection.

It's recommended to spend at least 30 minutes with a cat you're interested in adopting. If the shelter has a visitation room, you can settle in and wait for the cat to warm up to you. Rather than reaching out toward a potentially timid animal, wait for the cat to approach you for affection. For a confident Ragdoll, it will only take a moment, but more nervous cats may need more time before they feel comfortable with you. Do not pick up a cat that you aren't familiar with. If the cat is comfortable with your presence, you can try playing with a wand toy or string to see how playful and energetic the cat may be. This can be helpful in evaluating whether the Ragdoll will fit in with your family and other pets.

The first few weeks with your new Ragdoll will be discussed in a later chapter, but remember that it may take several weeks after adoption for your cat to fully come out of its shell. There will be a decompression period where your cat may be nervous or shy, but this is simply a natural reaction to moving into a new home. After some time settling in, the cat's previously friendly personality will return.

Photo Courtesy of Angie Winstead

CHAPTER 4

All About Ragdoll Breeders

Finding a Reputable Breeder

> "
>
> *The best way to choose a Ragdoll breeder is by referral. Ask a breeder if you can make contact with previous clients, or even with the veterinarians they regularly use for exams and vaccines. The breeder that you choose should be in good standing with cat organizations and easy to contact. By that, I mean that they should be willing to discuss your questions or concerns over the phone. Also, do not choose your Ragdoll kitten from a breeder that will not allow you to pick up your kitten from their home—this is a big red flag.*
>
> MELISSA FIRESTONE
> *Rockstar Ragdolls*
>
> "

When purchasing a Ragdoll cat, it's important to work with reputable breeders to ensure that you're getting a healthy purebred animal. Cat associations, such as the Cat Fanciers Association (CFA), Cat Fanciers' Federation (CFF), and The International Cat Association (TICA), maintain a list of registered breeders on their websites. These lists are a great place to start your search. Breed clubs such as the Ragdoll Fanciers' Club also maintain lists of breeders.

Photo Courtesy of Melissa Firestone - Rockstar Ragdolls

It's best to avoid classified ad websites, as reputable breeders would not advertise their cats there. Breeders who are not registered with any cat association should also be avoided, as they cannot provide pedigrees for any of the kittens they produce. The kittens may be purebred, but without pedigree papers, it's impossible to prove.

Unfortunately, finding the right breeder is not as simple as choosing one from the list. Once you've found a registered Ragdoll breeder in your desired area, you should do some research to confirm that they are ethical. The first thing to check for is health testing, which will be discussed in more detail in the next section. Additionally, ethical breeders do not breed on a large scale and should not have large numbers of kittens available. Large-scale breeders are considered mills and are unlikely to produce healthy, quality Ragdolls. A good breeder will only have one or two litters at a time to ensure that each kitten gets enough attention and human interaction.

When choosing a purebred cat breeder, it's crucial to find a breeder that follows the breed standard. The breed standard, which will be

HELPFUL TIP
Health Testing

Responsible Ragdoll breeders should perform regular health and genetic testing on cats in their breeding program. Examples of tests that should be run on Ragdolls include screening for hypertrophic cardiomyopathy (HCM), mucopolysaccharidosis VI (MPS VI), and polycystic kidney disease (PKD), several conditions known to affect this breed. This testing is usually done through a genetic marker report ordered by a veterinarian.

discussed in detail in a later chapter, ensures that a breed maintains a certain quality. However, following the breed standard does not mean all kittens will conform exactly. Even if two champion Ragdolls are bred, a few kittens may be show or breeding quality, but many will just be pet quality.

Be aware that once you find an ethical registered Ragdoll breeder, you will likely undergo some screening as well. A breeder will want to know more about you and your lifestyle to ensure that their kitten is going to a good home. You may need to answer questions about past and current cat ownership and experience, your daily schedule, family life, etc. They may also ask you about your experience with Ragdolls and whether you intend to keep the cat indoors or outdoors as well. It's important not to get defensive if you feel that the breeder is being intrusive. They simply want to make sure their beloved kittens are going to homes that will properly care for them.

Health Tests and Certifications

An ethical breeder should health test all cats prior to breeding to ensure that they are not passing down any genetic disorders and are producing the healthiest cats possible. Health testing is important not only for the individual cat you intend to bring home but the breed as a whole. By screening their breeding stock, ethical breeders can help eliminate serious health conditions from the gene pool and improve the overall health of the Ragdoll breed. At a minimum, an ethical breeder should be testing for hypertrophic cardiomyopathy, polycystic kidney disease, progressive retinal atrophy, feline leukemia virus, and feline immuno-deficiency virus.

Hypertrophic cardiomyopathy (HCM) is a serious heart condition that affects cats of all breeds, including those without a pedigree. This disease causes the walls of the heart to thicken, which decreases the heart's ability to pump blood throughout the body. Although HCM is more prevalent in certain breeds, it can affect any cat. Genetic testing is available to determine whether certain cats are at an increased risk of developing the disorder. However, HCM cannot be formally diagnosed without an echo-cardiogram. Once diagnosed, HCM can be managed but is not curable.

Polycystic kidney disease (PKD) is not common in Ragdolls but is more prevalent in non-traditionally colored Ragdolls that have Persians or other outcrosses in their pedigrees. As the name suggests, the condition causes multiple cysts to form inside the kidneys. The cysts are often present from birth and continue to grow larger over time. Eventually, they will disrupt the function of the kidneys and cause the cat to develop kidney failure. Genetic tests are available to determine if a cat has the defective PKD1 gene that causes the disease. Again, affected cats can be treated, but the disease is not curable.

Progressive retinal atrophy (PRA) is an eye condition that causes the retina to degenerate over time, resulting in blindness. There are two forms of the disease: early-onset and late-onset. The early-onset form is typically inherited, and affected cats are usually diagnosed around two to three months of age. The late-onset form doesn't usually affect cats until they are between two and five years of age. Again, PRA is not common in Ragdolls, but it is common in Persians. Nontraditional Ragdolls and those with Persian outcrosses in their pedigree should undergo genetic testing for PRA before being bred.

Feline leukemia virus (FeLV) is a common viral disease that affects cats of all breeds. It's estimated that between 2 and 3% of all cats in the United States are infected with FeLV. The disease is caused by a retrovirus that weakens the cat's immune system, potentially putting them at risk for contracting other fatal diseases. It's usually passed from cat to cat through saliva or nasal secretions. Like FeLV, feline immunodeficiency virus (FIV) is a common disease that affects up to 4% of all cats in the United States. It is similar to human immunodeficiency virus (HIV) in its effect. Like HIV, FIV weakens the immune system and cannot be cured. Affected cats may eventually develop feline AIDS (acquired immunodeficiency syndrome), which can be fatal. It's important to note that FIV and feline AIDS cannot be transferred to humans, only other cats. To prevent these diseases from being passed on, ethical breeders should test all adult cats in the home before producing any litters.

Since ethical breeders are willing to put so much time, money, and effort into the production of healthy kittens, they typically offer a genetic health guarantee. The guarantee is often two or three years, but some may be longer. This means that if your Ragdoll kitten is diagnosed with a hereditary condition, your breeder will provide you with a healthy replacement kitten or refund, whichever is agreed upon in the contract.

Breeder Contracts and Guarantees

> "
>
> *Breeding responsibly is about much more than just putting two cats together and having kittens. A responsible breeder should have genetic tests done on all breeding cats and be willing to take video calls to prove that they are a legit breeder with actual kittens. A responsible breeder will keep kittens until they are at least 12 to 14 weeks of age; this ensures that the kittens will leave with at least two sets of vaccinations and will have gotten proper socialization with mom and siblings, as well as human socialization with the breeder. Finding a breeder that you feel comfortable communicating with is important. As your kitten grows, you may have questions or concerns that your breeder can help with.*
>
> STORMI NELL
> *Familytime Rags*
>
> "

When buying a Ragdoll from a reputable breeder, you will likely need to sign a contract before bringing your new companion home. The contract is a legally binding document, so it's important to read it thoroughly before signing. The purpose of the contract is to prioritize the health and well-being of the kitten while also protecting both the breeder and buyer. Each breeder will have different terms in their contract, so again, read it thoroughly and ask questions before signing anything.

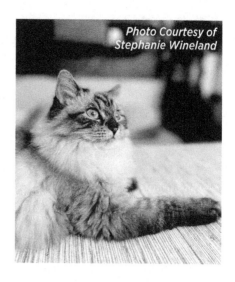

Photo Courtesy of Stephanie Wineland

It's common for breeders to include certain clauses about veterinary care. The breeder may ask that buyers agree not to declaw their cat due to the physical and emotional damage the procedure can cause. If the cat has not yet been spayed or neutered, there may be a statement about the appropriate age for altering. Additionally, the contract may stipulate that the owners must keep up with routine veterinary care such as vaccinations and deworming.

The contract may also state any short- and long-term health guarantees offered by the breeder. As stated in an earlier section, many breeders offer genetic health guarantees for a certain period of the cat's life. They may also offer short-term guarantees regarding the kitten's overall health upon leaving the breeder's home. However, many short-term guarantees depend on quarantining the cat away from other animals for a short period after arriving at their new home.

A breeder's contract may also state what should happen to the cat if you are no longer able to provide it with a home. Reputable breeders generally ask that you return the cat to them rather than attempt to rehome it yourself or drop it off at a shelter.

Remember, if there is anything in the contract that you do not agree with, it's important that you discuss the matter with the breeder before signing it. If you end up breaking the terms of the contract, you could potentially find yourself facing a lawsuit. However, most breeders are happy to discuss the terms of their contract with buyers to make sure that everyone is on the same page.

Choosing Your Perfect Kitten

> " When choosing your Ragdoll, it is important to ensure the cat is healthy in appearance and well socialized. The cat should have bright, clear eyes, be confident, alert, and have a plush, bunny-soft coat free from mats or tangles. You should ensure that the cat has been examined by a licensed veterinarian and has all age-appropriate vaccinations. Ideally, the cat will be spayed or neutered, and its parents will have genetically tested negative for polycystic kidney disease (PKD) and hypertrophic cardiomyopathy (HCM).
>
> EMILY BREZINA
> *PrettyPurrs Ragdoll Cattery* "

Once you've found an ethical Ragdoll breeder, you may have a number of kittens to choose from. If you are able to visit the breeder's home to meet the kittens before purchasing, you may consider making a list of your preferred characteristics. Although most Ragdolls will have a similar temperament overall, each kitten will have its own unique personality traits. Do you prefer an active and outgoing cat, or would you prefer one that would rather cuddle all day? Do you mind if the kitten is a little shy with strangers? It's easy to get wrapped up in a kitten's appearance, but it's important not to be swayed by a cat's beauty if its personality doesn't work well with your household.

If your breeder is not local, you may need to work together

Photo Courtesy of
Amanda Souza-PurrrfectDollz

to determine which kitten would suit your lifestyle best. You may have already had in-depth discussions with the breeder about what characteristics you're looking for in a Ragdoll. If you are not able to meet the kittens beforehand, you may want to rely on your breeder's expertise and knowledge of their cats. In many cases, you will end up with a better match than if you had chosen yourself.

Adopting Multiple Cats

If you have the budget and the room to bring home more than one Ragdoll, it can be beneficial to adopt multiple kittens. Cats are social animals, and although they enjoy human companionship, they will often be happier with a feline friend. In fact, many breeders and rescue organizations recommend adopting cats in pairs for this very reason.

When you adopt a kitten, it will likely be the first time the kitten has been away from its mom and littermates. Moving into a new household can be incredibly stressful, but it can be easier with a sibling. With two or more kittens, you won't need to worry about your new cat getting bored while you're at work. Ragdolls can be somewhat demanding of your time and attention, and a playmate can help keep your kitten busy while you are away or doing household chores.

If you already have another cat at home, you may not need to consider bringing home siblings. However, if the other cat is much older, it may not be a good match for a playful and energetic kitten. It can be stressful for older cats to experience the demanding nature of an overly enthusiastic kitten. Having a more age-appropriate playmate can help keep the new kitten busy without harassing the older cat.

Bringing home multiple cats can make your life easier in some ways, but it can be more difficult in others. You will need to be prepared to feed, groom, and clean up after two kittens. Your monthly litter and food expenses will double, as will veterinary bills. It's important that you spend time with each kitten individually to develop a bond, so make sure you have the time and budget before bringing them home.

CHAPTER 5

Preparing for Your Ragdoll Cat

> "
>
> *One trick I tell my clients if they have another cat at home is to get the scent of the other cat on a dry washcloth—you can get good scent from the sides of their cheeks/mouths and belly. After wiping down the kitten with a fresh damp cloth, take the cloth with the other cat's scent and wipe it on the kitten's head and back. If the kitten smells like your other cat, they will accept him faster.*
>
> ROCHELLE REXIUS
> *VegasRagdolls*
>
> "

Necessary Supplies

Before you bring your new Ragdoll home for the first time, it's recommended to have all the necessary supplies ready at home. That way, you can focus on getting your kitten settled without worrying about running to the pet store for last-minute items. If you have other cats in your home, you may already have most of the supplies you need. However, since you will need to keep your Ragdoll separated from your other pets at first, you may need to pick up a few extra items. If this will be your first cat, consider putting together a shopping list before heading to your local pet store or favorite online retailer.

First, you'll need a way to transport your new cat from the breeder or shelter to your home. A soft-sided or plastic pet carrier is the most commonly used method. It's not recommended to carry the cat in your arms on the way home. Many cats get nervous in the car, and you don't want a panicked cat trying to escape the vehicle. The quiet, enclosed space of a pet carrier typically helps keep nervous cats calm and prevents injuries to you and the cat.

Photo Courtesy of Lindsay Fontaine

One of the most important items on the list is food. You will need to find out what the breeder or rescue is feeding their cats so you can purchase the same food. Even if you don't intend to feed that type of food long-term, you will need some to help transition your Ragdoll to the new diet. Switching too quickly can cause digestive upset, so it's recommended to transition over the course of several days. Don't forget bowls for your new cat's food and water. Many cat owners prefer flat food dishes to reduce whisker fatigue. Some cats also prefer drinking out of fountains rather than bowls, but many will stay hydrated using just a bowl.

Another crucial item to purchase is a litter box and litter. Your options for this will be discussed thoroughly in Chapter 8. Again, if you have other cats, you may already have litter, but you will need to set up a separate box for your Ragdoll. After your new feline friend has adjusted to life in your home, you may encourage him to use your existing litter boxes, but you will need a separate box for the first few weeks. Accidents can happen, so you may want to consider buying a stain and odor-removing cleaning product as well.

You will also need to make sure your Ragdoll is comfortable, so make sure you have a bed for him. There are many different kinds of cat beds on the market, and cats often prefer one type over another, but you'll have to take your best guess until you get to know your Ragdoll

HELPFUL TIP

Go Fetch!

Ragdolls are easily trainable and love to learn new games with their humans. So when preparing your home for a new Ragdoll kitten, ensure you provide plenty of toys for mental stimulation. Many Ragdoll owners report that their cats love playing fetch and hide-and-seek with their humans. While teaching your cat to play fetch may be more complex than training a dog to do the same, with patience and dedication, you and your cat could enjoy a fetch game in a few weeks.

better. Nervous kittens may prefer a covered bed to provide them with a sense of comfort and security.

To prevent your Ragdoll from damaging your furniture, you should also have a scratching post ready. Again, some cats prefer different scratching surfaces, so you'll need to get to know your Ragdoll to determine what type of cat furniture to invest in. This may not be a necessary item for the first few days, but you will need it eventually. You may also want to invest in furniture protectors if you have furniture that you would prefer not to be scratched.

Small but necessary items include toys to keep your kitten occupied. Catnip toys are generally enjoyed by most. A brush to keep your Ragdoll's coat mat-free is also required. Although Ragdoll kittens don't have an abundance of fur, it's recommended to get them used to the grooming process as early as possible. Treats are also a good idea to help train your kitten and encourage him to interact with you if he's shy or nervous.

You may also want to consider buying a calming pheromone spray or diffuser. This can help reduce stress for both your kitten and any existing cats. If using a spray, be sure to read the label, as some products must be applied every so often. Diffusers usually plug into the wall and dispense pheromones for a certain duration, typically 30 days or so. Calming products won't guarantee that the introduction of your new cat will go well, but it can help to reduce tension as the cats get to know each other.

A breakaway collar and ID tag are optional items but are highly recommended if your Ragdoll will be spending any time outdoors. Some owners prefer their cats wear identification in the house just in case they slip through an open door, while others prefer to only have a collar on if the cat is outside. The collar should be one that breaks away with slight pressure to prevent your cat from being injured if the collar gets caught on anything. The ID tag should have your contact information so your Ragdoll can be returned to you if he gets lost. If you don't want your Ragdoll to have unsupervised time outside, you can also consider a harness and leash. This will allow your cat to explore the outdoors safely with you by his side. If you plan on taking your Ragdoll outside, flea and tick prevention products are also recommended.

Although many Ragdolls prefer to spend most of their time on the floor rather than on elevated surfaces, you can expect your curious new cat to jump up occasionally. You can provide your cat with his own elevated spaces with a cat tree or cat shelves. Some owners even go as far as placing elevated spaces in every room so their Ragdolls have plenty of climbing options. If you have shelves or counters with precious items, consider using museum putty. Cats are notoriously fond of knocking things off shelves, and museum putty can be used to gently hold your belongings in place.

Dental care is important for any cat, so you may want to purchase a few products to help keep your Ragdoll's teeth clean and healthy. A toothbrush and toothpaste are a great way to maintain your cat's dental health, but you'll want to spend time getting him used to the process. If you'd prefer a less invasive method of teeth cleaning, consider buying dental treats. These treats are typically extra crunchy to help scrape off plaque and tartar while also freshening your cat's breath.

As a quick reminder, here are the supplies you should consider having on hand for the arrival of your Ragdoll cat.

Necessary Supplies
- Pet carrier
- Food
- Food and water bowls
- Litter box
- Litter
- Bed
- Scratching post
- Toys
- Brush
- Treats

Optional Supplies
- Water fountain
- Calming pheromone spray
- Museum putty
- Collar and ID tag
- Harness
- Cat tree or shelves
- Furniture protectors
- Flea and tick control
- Stain and odor remover
- Dental care products

Preparing Your Other Pets

> **"**
>
> *Current pets can 'meet' the new kitten or cat through the safety of a door. After a few days, allow the new kitten to venture out of its safe area on its own. In the beginning, supervision with other pets is important. Don't worry if your new (or current) pet gets stressed—you can always bring the new baby back to the safe room and try again later. Slow introductions are best for less stress.*
>
> STORMI NELL
> *Familytime Rags*
>
> **"**

For the first few days or weeks, it's recommended to separate your new Ragdoll from your other pets. The introductory period can be stressful, and a temporary separation keeps all animals safe and as stress-free as possible. The length of time you separate the animals will depend on the pets involved. Some pets may get used to each other within a few days, while others may take a few weeks to warm up to each other. By closely observing their behavior, you can estimate the best time to remove any barriers. Fearful or aggressive introductions can set the tone for the relationship between your pets, so try to introduce them gradually in as calm a manner as possible.

At first, you may want a solid barrier, such as a door, between the pets. The animals will still be aware of each other's presence but won't be able to interact directly. If all goes well with a solid barrier, you can try using a baby gate. Since many cats will effortlessly hop over even the tallest baby gate, consider using two pressure-mounted gates to block the doorway.

You may want to give your Ragdoll a chance to settle in for the first day or two, but you can begin introducing your existing pets by swapping bedding. Place your pets' bedding in an area accessible to your Ragdoll so that he can experience the scents without the stress of a face-to-face meeting. Likewise, you can take some of your Ragdoll's bedding and place it in an area where your existing pets can investigate it. You can also

Photo Courtesy of Audrey Bodnar

consider temporarily switching their living areas. Your existing pets can spend time in the area you set aside for your Ragdoll, and your Ragdoll can have access to the rest of the house.

If you've progressed to using a see-through barrier, your pets will be able to have some face-to-face interaction but without the ability to seriously injure each other should something go wrong. The first few face-to-face meetings should be supervised so that you can intervene if necessary. Spraying the barrier with a calming pheromone spray or offering treats can help ease tension.

If you are introducing your Ragdoll to other cats, be sure to go as slow as necessary. When there is no more hissing, growling, or spitting, the cats are ready to be introduced without a barrier. Remember, it's possible that there may still be conflict, so supervise closely. Never force cats to interact or move them closer to each other, as this can cause a fight. If the cats do not interact once the barrier is removed, let them be. They will get to know each other on their own time. If the cats appear to get along, it's still important to observe them closely for the first few weeks to watch for signs of bullying.

Extra caution should be taken when introducing a new cat to any dog. Even dogs who are normally friendly to cats can give chase if the cat runs. If the dog manages to catch the cat, serious and even fatal injuries can

Photo Courtesy of
Denice Fisher

occur in the blink of an eye. Always err on the side of caution and consider having your dog on a leash during introductions. It can be helpful to provide your new cat with elevated surfaces or special access to areas away from the dog. Many cats live happily with dogs, but felines enjoy having their own space to retreat to when needed.

Preparing Your Children and Family

You should begin preparing your children long before you bring your new Ragdoll home. It can be tempting to surprise them with a new pet, but the excitement of surprise is often frightening and stressful for the cat. A frightened cat may lash out and scratch or bite to defend itself. It's recommended to have a discussion before the cat arrives about appropriate behavior around the new cat. This conversation can be as in-depth as necessary, depending on the age of your kids. Remember, this conversation is about the cat's comfort and safety, as well as the children's.

Teach your children to let the cat approach them first and to behave calmly so that they don't scare the cat. You may also want to discourage them from picking the cat up, especially if you are bringing home a kitten. With excitable younger children, you may need to intervene and try the introduction later when the children are calmer.

You should also teach your kids how to safely interact with a new cat. Speaking softly and moving slowly are best, especially with a nervous cat. Explain that there are certain areas of the cat's body that are okay to touch, such as the head and back, while other areas, like the tail and tummy, should be avoided. To encourage safe and fun interaction, have your child offer a few treats to the cat. Again, calm and quiet behavior should be encouraged. As the cat gets to know the children, they can try playing with it with a string or wand toy.

It can be helpful to provide your new cat with areas away from the kids that he can retreat to if he feels overwhelmed. Be sure to supervise any interactions between the cat and children to ensure that everyone is being respectful. Supervision is crucial to prevent injuries to both the cat and children.

Kitten-Proofing Your Home

> **"**
>
> *When preparing for a Ragdoll, or any other kitten, it's helpful to remember that they will get into everything. Make sure that your electrical cords are out of the way—cords that can't be put out of reach can be placed inside a tube to prevent chewing. For things like a surge protector, there are cable management boxes that you can buy on Amazon that work well. You'll also want to secure screens on windows, keep toilet seats down, store plastic bags and harmful chemicals inside a childproof cabinet, and check with your vet about any houseplants that you have—there are many, many poisonous houseplants that people are unaware of.*
>
> STORMI NELL
> *Familytime Rags*
>
> **"**

Ragdoll kittens are inquisitive creatures, so before your new companion arrives, you'll want to go through your home and remove any potential dangers. As your Ragdoll matures and understands the rules of the house, you can be a little less cautious, but for the first few months, it's important to prioritize safety.

Begin your kitten-proofing process by picking up small objects around the home that could be tempting to a curious kitten. Small items, such as children's toys, game pieces, hair ties, crayons, and plastic bags, can all be potential dangers to a kitten if swallowed. Placing these items in a container with a lid is recommended.

Some houseplants can be toxic for cats, so it's important to verify that the plants you have in your home are safe. Popular houseplants that are toxic to cats include croton, philodendron, ficus, monstera, and poinsettia. These plants can cause a range of issues, from digestive upset and vomiting to seizures and even death. The ASPCA has a complete list of common plants that are toxic to cats on its website.

It's also important to keep your kitten out of tempting but dangerous spaces such as trash cans, cupboards, and laundry bins. You may also want to consider installing childproof locks on any cabinets containing dangerous items such as medication or cleaning and beauty supplies. Washing machines and dryers also present a danger to kittens, so it's important to keep the doors closed when not in use and check inside before starting your wash. Many kittens have been seriously injured or killed after taking a nap in these spaces.

Photo Courtesy of Amanda Carter

Secure all windows and window screens that your kitten may be able to access. A rambunctious kitten can easily knock out a loose window screen, and the resulting fall could result in serious injury. If your windows do not have screens on them, it's best to keep them closed. Any ground-level windows should be kept closed as well. Although your Ragdoll likely won't be injured from a fall, he could escape and fall victim to one of the many dangers outdoors. For this reason, it's also important to continually make sure any doors to the outside do not get left open.

You may also consider removing tempting items temporarily. This may include curtains and any expensive or sentimental decorations or furniture.

The First Few Weeks

During the first few weeks after you've brought your Ragdoll home, you'll want to begin establishing your daily routines. You can begin the introduction process if you have other pets or children in the home and work on socialization as well. Additionally, it's recommended to make an appointment with your vet within the first few days of ownership so that the kitten can be examined and vaccinated as necessary.

Photo Courtesy of Sherry Goeben

Remember, this period can be stressful for both you and your Ragdoll. As you get to know each other, take a deep breath and understand that this period is temporary. This may be your kitten's first time away from its mother and littermates, so stress is normal. Your kitten may be more fearful, withdrawn, or sassy than usual, but it's important to go slow and not overwhelm him.

> *I recommend starting the kitten out in a smaller area for the first week or so while it's adapting to its new home. Most kittens tend to be frightened the first day or two, so create a calm environment and give the kitten lots of love. Feed it the foods that were recommended by the breeder and use the same type of cat litter that the kitten used at the breeder's home to help ease the transition.*
>
> ANN J. LANG
> *Starliterags*

If your kitten does not seem interested in food or using the litter box, it can be helpful to give him some time alone. Some cats are too nervous to eat or relieve themselves in a new space if they feel they are being watched. You may wake in the morning to find that your cat has emptied the food dish and used the litter box while you were sleeping. The same is true if your kitten seeks out tight spaces to rest. That comfortable bed you bought him may be too exposed for his current level of comfort, so don't be offended if he instead chooses to sleep under your bed or behind the sofa.

After a few weeks, your Ragdoll's personality should begin to emerge, and his behavior should return to normal. Remember, kittens sleep around 20 hours per day, so it's important to give your Ragdoll plenty of space to relax in a comfortable place of his own. It can be tempting to interact with a new pet frequently, but let your cat dictate your level of interaction during the first few weeks. As he gets more comfortable, he'll likely begin seeking attention more often.

CHAPTER 6

Caring for Your Ragdoll Cat

Indoor or Outdoor

There are many aspects to consider when deciding whether your Ragdoll should be an indoor-only cat or have outdoor access as well. One of the main reasons many owners choose to allow their cats outside is to provide the cat with mental stimulation. However, cats that spend a significant amount of time outside are at a higher risk for illnesses and injuries.

Indoor cats tend to be less active and require more focused attention from their owners to meet their mental and physical exercise needs. Weight-related medical conditions, such as obesity, arthritis, and heart disease, are more common in indoor-only cats. Boredom-related behavioral issues, such as scratching and urinating outside of the litter box, are also more common.

Outdoor cats tend to lead more fulfilling but often shorter lives. They are exposed to a number of dangers, including other cats, wildlife, and people. Injuries, parasites, and diseases such as FIV, feline leukemia, and rabies are more common in outdoor cats. They are also at risk of being hit by cars and ingesting toxic substances such as antifreeze or rodent poison. Without proper identification, such as a collar or microchip, it's also possible that your cat may be picked up by someone who believes the cat is lost.

To provide your cat with the entertainment offered by the outdoors but without the risk, consider setting up safe observation areas. You can set up bird or squirrel feeders outside the window to bring wildlife into

Photo Courtesy of
Denice Fisher

view. If you have the space and budget, you can also consider building your cat a "catio," which is an outdoor enclosure that can be accessed by a window or pet door. Catios are a great way for your Ragdoll to explore the outdoors without being exposed to potential dangers. If your cat feels unsafe for any reason, he can simply go back inside the house. Plus, you won't have to worry about any wildlife following him indoors as you might with just a pet door. You can also teach your cat to walk on a leash and harness. That way, he can explore the outdoors with you by his side to take him home when he's ready.

If you do choose to allow your Ragdoll outdoors, it's important to take precautions to keep him safe. Be sure to get your cat microchipped so that you can be contacted should he get lost. A breakaway collar with an identification tag is also a smart choice. For outdoor cats, it's crucial to stay up to date on vaccinations and flea and tick prevention. The diseases and parasites your cat may be exposed to will vary by location, so ask your

HEALTH ALERT!

Hairball Supplements

Ragdoll cats are known for their long, luscious fur, but this luxurious coat can have its drawbacks: hairballs. Grooming your cat plays a large part in preventing hairballs, but certain supplements may also encourage your cat's digestive system to pass hairballs more easily. These supplements include catnip, cat grass, psyllium seed, and other specially formulated treats. Always speak with your vet before providing supplements.

veterinarian which product will best protect your Ragdoll.

It's also important to mention that cats can have a significantly harmful effect on local native wildlife. According to the American Bird Conservancy, domestic cats are the single biggest threat to birds in North America. In the United States, it's estimated that cats kill over two billion birds each year. Even the most well-fed cat will happily hunt and kill birds and other small animals when given the opportunity. As invasive predators, felines can have dire consequences for threatened and endangered species.

Before you allow your Ragdoll outdoors, you may also want to check the contract you signed with the breeder. Many breeders do not want their cats exposed to the potential dangers of the outdoors, and doing so may violate the agreements in their contract.

Emotional Needs

> *Never force your kitten to be held or cuddled. To form the best possible bond with your kitten, respect its space and just be present with it. Talk softly to the kitten and encourage interaction through treats or toys.*
>
> EMILY BREZINA
> *PrettyPurrs Ragdoll Cattery*

When welcoming a Ragdoll cat into your home, it's important to meet your new companion's physical needs by providing him with a high-quality diet and plenty of exercise opportunities. However, you should also be prepared to meet your Ragdoll's emotional needs to ensure he has a happy and fulfilling life with you.

Photo Courtesy of Carole Scott

Every cat will have unique emotional needs. Some cats may be more independent and prefer to meet their own needs, while others may be more reliant on you to keep them entertained and happy. Not all cats thrive on attention and need to interact with their people throughout the day.

During the first few weeks with your Ragdoll, don't be surprised if your new cat isn't particularly affectionate or reliant on you for care. Many cats need a period of adjustment, and they may not yet be comfortable enough with you to request affection. As your new companion warms up to you, he may begin spending more time with you and feel more confident demanding attention. As stated in an earlier chapter, Ragdolls can be very demanding and require a lot of attention. Be sure to schedule plenty of cuddle and playtime into your daily schedule to make sure you're meeting your cat's emotional needs.

A Safe Retreat

As previously mentioned, many Ragdolls are outgoing and want to spend every moment with their favorite people. Some cats may demand attention at certain times of the day and otherwise choose to spend their time alone or with other cats. Depending on your cat's personality, he may need just a few hours alone to recharge his social battery, or he

Photo Courtesy of
Vickie Hatfield

may spend much of the day enter-
taining himself. Regardless of your
Ragdoll's social habits, it's important to provide him with a private
space to retreat to when needed.

A safe retreat is especially
important if you have children or
other pets in the home. It's especially important to teach children
that if the cat is in his own des-
ignated space, he should be left
alone to rest. This rule applies to
adults as well. It's more difficult to
tell other pets to leave their companion alone, but elevated spaces
generally deter dogs and often
other cats. Cats without safe spaces may lash out or develop behavioral
problems due to stress.

The space you set up for your Ragdoll will depend on the available
space in your home. If you are short on space, consider setting up an elevated and secluded area for your cat. A cat tree with an enclosed section
or a cat shelf may be just what your cat needs. It's recommended to set
up any cat furniture in a quiet area where the cat can still watch household activities without being actively involved. If you have more space
available, you can decide what room your cat would be most comfortable
retreating to and set up his space there. If possible, consider setting up
an area near a window where your cat can rest and observe the world
from the comfort of his safe place.

Hairballs

As a long-haired breed, Ragdolls are more prone to hairballs than
many breeds. Regardless of coat length, most cats develop hairballs on
occasion, and it's generally nothing to worry about. During the self-grooming process, cats remove loose hair with their tongues and sometimes

swallow it. The accumulation of this hair in their digestive system is called a hairball. As the hair builds up in the stomach, the cat may vomit up the hairball to remove it. However, some hair will pass through the cat's digestive system without issue. If too much hair tries to pass through the digestive system, it could potentially cause a blockage.

Most cats get hairballs as infrequently as once per month or less. Long-haired breeds, such as Ragdolls, can develop hairballs more frequently. If you notice your Ragdoll bringing up hairballs often, you may want to discuss it with your vet, as it can be a symptom of gastrointestinal issues. More frequent hairballs can also be a symptom of overgrooming, which can be caused by stress.

When cats cough up hairballs, they can appear to be gagging or choking, and they may stretch their necks out in an attempt to remove the hairball from their stomach. This behavior can be alarming, but it is perfectly normal and does not require human intervention. There are many products on the market designed to help hairballs move through the cat's body more efficiently, but they are generally unnecessary unless recommended by your vet. Most cats can handle hairballs without any help.

If you choose to use a hairball product, it's best to follow the instructions on the label as closely as possible to make sure you are using it correctly. If you would prefer not to use an oil- or lubricant-based product, you may want to consider a hairball cat food. Hairball kibble is usually high in fiber to help hair move more efficiently through the digestive system.

The only time hairballs can be a concern is if your cat continuously struggles to pass them. Repeated retching and a loss of energy or appetite is a concern and should be addressed by a veterinarian as soon as possible.

Photo Courtesy of
Sabrina Kapsa - Kingstondolls

Enrichment and Playtime

> "
> *Ragdolls can get much bigger than the average cat, so you'll need a cat tree that is sturdy enough. A lot of really cute structures designed for smaller cats aren't going to survive very long with Ragdolls. A lot of my cats like to be high up, so picking a cat tree that's tall is also important.*
>
> PAM BANTA
> *Lightfoot Ragdolls*
> "

As mentioned earlier in the chapter, enrichment and playtime are essential parts of maintaining your Ragdoll's physical and mental well-being. This is especially true for indoor-only cats. In the wild, cats spend up to six hours per day hunting, which satisfies their need for physical exercise and mental stimulation. Domestic cats need daily enrichment and play as a replacement. Cats that spend time outdoors can also benefit from daily playtime. Some sources suggest that play reduces the amount of time outdoor cats spend hunting prey, thereby reducing their effect on local wildlife populations. Additionally, playtime helps strengthen the bond between you and your Ragdoll.

When playing with your Ragdoll, always let him set the pace. If he prefers a slow-speed chase along the floor with a wand toy, don't try to force him into fast and aerobatic play. Not all cats enjoy the same play style. Some may prefer wand toys, while others enjoy chasing lasers. Choose the play style and toy that your Ragdoll likes best. Many cat owners recommend ending the play session by allowing the cat to catch and carry away the toy or by giving him a treat. This action simulates the satisfaction of a successful hunt and will encourage your cat to play again next time.

In addition to play sessions, you can keep a food-motivated cat entertained with puzzle toys. Puzzle toys are typically filled with your cat's favorite treat or regular food and must be manipulated in a certain way to release the tasty morsels inside. If you are interested in using puzzle toys as enrichment, it can be helpful to purchase a few so you can swap them out occasionally to prevent boredom. However, if you're on a budget, you can also create your own puzzle toys by using items around your house. Sprinkle treats into a pizza box with holes cut into it, and you have a low-cost DIY puzzle toy. You can also fill a larger box with crumpled-up paper, toilet paper tubes, or even socks or small towels. A few treats hidden among the paper or fabric will keep your cat entertained while you accomplish your daily chores.

Photo Courtesy of Mercedes Maze

Cat exercise wheels are also great products for keeping indoor cats fit. They are similar to the wheels placed in rodent cages but are a more appropriate size for cats. These kitty treadmills can be expensive, typically a few hundred dollars, but they are ideal for keeping your Ragdoll fit and busy. Since they are safe for cats to use on their own, you don't need to be present. Your cat can simply step onto the wheel and run as fast or slow as he likes.

An enriching environment is crucial for any indoor cat. Interacting and playing with your cat should be part of your daily routine, but even providing your cat with something as simple as a birdfeeder outside a window can help to prevent boredom-related behavioral problems. The more physical and mental activity options you can incorporate into your cat's daily routine, the happier he will be. Just remember that mentally stimulating activities can be exhausting, and your Ragdoll will likely need a relaxing nap afterward.

CHAPTER 7

Training and Socialization

The Importance of Socialization

The process of socialization involves acclimating your Ragdoll to the sights, smells, and sounds of life with humans. A well-socialized cat is accustomed to and generally enjoys spending time with people. An unsocialized cat, on the other hand, will actively avoid interactions with people. Feral cats who rarely have contact with humans are on one side of the socialization spectrum, while the friendliest of household cats

are on the other. Most cats are somewhere in the middle of this spectrum, but there are steps you can take to socialize your Ragdoll, whether he is a kitten or an adult. In general, kittens are easier to socialize than adult cats simply because they are more open to new experiences and have not yet developed negative attitudes toward people.

Socialization is important because most people want a cat that they can regularly share affection and play with. Well-socialized cats are safer to live with and are easier to han-

HELPFUL TIP

A Family Friendly Feline

These fluffy felines are known for their affectionate nature and love for humans. Ragdolls are also very playful and intelligent and love to learn new games. These traits make them excellent candidates for homes with small children. In addition, many owners report that Ragdolls tend to get along well with dogs and other cats in the home. Though generally laid-back in nature, the Ragdoll's large size can help them stand up to dogs who are still learning boundaries when it comes to cats.

dle for veterinary care and grooming. An unsocialized cat may behave aggressively out of fear when handled, which can be dangerous to both the cat and the handler.

To set your Ragdoll up for success, it's important to begin socialization as soon as you bring your new companion home. During the first few weeks, your Ragdoll will need time to decompress and get used to his new home, but you can still take steps to get him used to living in a home with a human family.

How to Socialize Your Ragdoll

When socializing your Ragdoll, it's important that you never force him to tolerate any experience. If he reacts out of fear, give him more space and go more slowly the next time. If you force your cat into certain interactions, he may react badly or develop negative associations. There are some situations where you will need to give your Ragdoll extra time to adapt. Remember, there is no set timeline for socialization, and it is a process that will need to continue throughout your cat's life. There is no reason to rush the socialization process.

First, you'll need to consider the experiences your cat is likely to have in your home. If you have children or frequent guests, you'll need to spend time introducing your cat to a variety of people and the noise levels, movements, and feelings associated with them. At first, you may need to get down on your Ragdoll's level. Use a calm, soothing voice and slow, deliberate movements. Treats are an excellent way to encourage your cat to approach new people and reward him for his bravery. If the cat seems scared or agitated, give him more space or take a break. Socialization sessions can be short, and you can do several throughout the day if needed.

Once your Ragdoll is comfortable being handled, you can begin getting him used to being handled by the vet or groomer. Gently touch him all over, going slowly in any areas where he exhibits signs of discomfort. You can try gently picking up each paw and extending each nail as you would when trimming his nails. Touch his ears as you would if you were looking inside them. You can also lift his lips to expose his teeth. As your cat becomes more comfortable with this handling, you can try

Photo Courtesy of Audrey Bodnar

running a brush over his coat. It's best to start on his back and gently work toward brushing more sensitive areas, such as the legs, belly, and tail.

Don't forget to expose your Ragdoll to sounds that he will hear while living in your home. Sounds such as the vacuum, music, or fireworks can be frightening to a cat that has never experienced them. There are many videos on YouTube that feature these sounds as a way to get animals used to them. You can begin playing the sound at a low volume and increase it slowly. Remember, treats will help encourage your Ragdoll to stay calm. If your cat becomes stressed at any point in a socialization session, it's best to back off and try again at a later time. There is no benefit to pushing a cat beyond his comfort threshold.

Training Your Ragdoll

> 66
>
> *Ragdolls are very motivated by food and affection and therefore highly trainable. When trying to prevent your cat from doing something that you don't want it to do, it's important to keep in mind that cats respond better to diversions than verbal commands. Cats do not respond to being disciplined; the general concept is 'for every no, there is a yes.' If you do not want your cat to scratch the furniture, you must provide an appropriate scratching surface for it to use nearby. Use a toy or a treat to calmly divert the cat's attention and reward it when it is in an appropriate location.*
>
> EMILY BREZINA
> *PrettyPurrs Ragdoll Cattery*
>
> 99

Training sessions should always be fun and engaging for your Ragdoll, so it's important to develop a training schedule. Try to schedule training sessions for times of the day when your cat is active and eager to interact. If you drag him out of bed for training sessions every day, he's not likely to enjoy the learning process. You should also try to train between mealtimes if possible. If your cat has just enjoyed a hearty meal, he probably won't want to work for more food.

To keep your Ragdoll engaged in training, try to use a high-value reward. Some cats may be willing to work for dry cat treats, while others may prefer a bit of cooked chicken breast. You may need to try out a few different kinds of treats to figure out which one your Ragdoll is most willing to work for. Cats that are highly food-motivated may be less picky, but you still want to make sure they are excited about the reward. Some

FAMOUS RAGDOLL

Mary Herbert's Cat

In 1972, Mary Ann Herbert, an Amer¬ican student, was released after more than three years held captive in communist China. While imprisoned she claimed that a cat had helped her keep her composure during her time in confinement. She expressed the desire to have a cat once she was released. When she returned home, she was gifted a Ragdoll cat to keep her company and help her acclimate.

cat owners save certain types of treats for training sessions so that their cats know they get something special when they participate in training.

Cats learn best when they are focused on and interested in interacting with you. For this reason, short training sessions are recommended. Younger cats may have less of an attention span, so you may want to limit sessions to just a few repetitions here and there. Older cats that are more experienced with the training process may be able to focus longer, but you should still keep the session short enough to end on a good note. With any training session, it's recommended to quit before your cat loses interest. For some, this may mean training sessions as short as one or two minutes.

While training your Ragdoll, it's best to work in environments with limited distractions at first. Without distractions, your cat can give you his undivided attention, and your training will have a higher rate of success. Once he fully understands what you're trying to teach him, you can begin introducing more distractions. If you want to show off your cat's tricks to your friends, it may be best to start with one or two people that your Ragdoll knows well before you ask him to perform in front of an audience.

To avoid frustrating or confusing your Ragdoll, try to focus on one skill at a time. For example, if you want to teach your cat to sit on command and give you a high five, it's best to work on the sit command until he fully understands what you're asking of him. Once he's learned that command, you can move on to teaching him the high five. If you try teaching both at the same time, your Ragdoll may not understand what you want him to do, which can lead to frustration and disinterest in training.

Be patient with your Ragdoll. Cats are individuals and learn at their own pace. More independent cats may take longer to train, and that's okay. Training should always be a positive experience for both the cat and the owner. If you ever find yourself getting frustrated with your cat's training progress, it may be time to take a break. If your cat doesn't understand what you're asking, you can also revert to a command that he knows well so that you can reward him and end the session on a positive note. The more positive you make each training experience, the more likely your cat is to engage with you in the future.

Clicker Training Basics

> "
> Ragdolls are a very intelligent breed and can easily learn what we call 'stupid dog tricks' using clicker training. Start by putting your kitty in a sitting position, then click and treat. Your Ragdoll will learn as quickly as your grandmother's poodle; however, please don't start your kitten on clicker training too early—I would recommend teaching your Ragdoll to sit with a clicker only after it's reached at least six months of age.
>
> BETTE WILLETTE
> *Willetteragdol*
> "

Clicker training is a form of positive reinforcement training that uses a clicker tool to mark the desired behavior. This training method has been used for decades, not only with cats but also with dogs, horses, and even dolphins. The value of clicker training is that the noise of the clicker marks the specific moment in time when your cat did what you asked. Clickers can be pressed quickly, so your cat won't need to wait for you to pull a treat out to understand that he did well and he will be getting a reward.

To begin clicker training your Ragdoll, you'll first need to "load" the clicker. A clicker does not inherently have any value to a cat; it's simply a tool that makes an interesting noise. You will need to teach your cat that the noise of the clicker means that a reward is on the way. To load the clicker, you simply need to gain your cat's attention, which shouldn't be

Photo Courtesy of Stormi Nell - FamilytimeRags

difficult if you've got a bag of treats. For the first session, simply press the clicker and immediately give your cat a treat. You can repeat this process a few times before ending the session. Depending on how quickly your cat picks up new behaviors, you may want to repeat the session several times over a number of days or weeks before moving on.

To teach your cat specific behaviors, it can be helpful to lure the cat into the desired behavior. For example, if you want to teach your cat to sit on command, you can lure him into position by holding a treat above his head. He will naturally need to sit to look up at the treat, though he may also try to grab it with his paws. Once his hind end touches the floor, press the clicker and reward him. You can also teach your cat targeting to help him learn specific behaviors. To do this, you'll need a targeting stick, which can either be made at home or purchased at a pet store or online retailer. Initially, you'll want to reward any interaction with the stick. The first time you introduce it and your cat touches it with his nose to investigate, click and reward. Eventually, you can use the stick to lure him into position or ask him to jump up, over, or through other objects.

As your Ragdoll progresses in his training, he'll quickly understand that the clicker means that he's done well and has earned a tasty reward. Eventually, he may even see you get the clicker out and begin offering behaviors in an effort to earn his favorite treat. Clicker training can be a great way to bond with your Ragdoll and provide him with plenty of physical and mental exercise.

Scratching and Bad Behavior

> **"**
>
> *Most Ragdoll kittens are surprisingly well-behaved, as far as kittens are concerned. They will already be litter-trained when you bring them home, but you'll want to provide them with several suitable scratching posts. You can teach your kitten to use the scratching post (rather than your furniture) by scratching on it with your fingers. Make sure to praise your kitten when it begins to scratch on the post!*
>
> ANN J. LANG
>
> *Starliterags*
>
> **"**

It's important to clarify that scratching is a natural instinctive behavior for cats. This behavior is used to mark objects with the cat's scent and to remove any dead or damaged parts of the claws. It's also a great stretch that helps to relieve stress. However, scratching can become an unwanted behavior when the cat begins damaging furniture or flooring. To limit the damage, it's important to provide your Ragdoll with acceptable places to scratch. If you want to prevent your cat from destroying your furniture, you need to provide him with scratching options that are more desirable than your sofa or table legs.

Most cats prefer scratching on taller objects. Since Ragdolls tend to be quite large cats, make sure that the cat furniture you purchase is tall enough for your cat to stretch as much as he'd like. This typically means a scratching post at least 32 inches in height. Any cat furniture you buy should also be sturdy, as any wobble may discourage your Ragdoll from using it. Many cats have preferences regarding the surface they scratch, so you may want to provide several options to determine which one your

Ragdoll likes best. Carpet, sisal rope, and corrugated cardboard are the most popular materials for cat scratching posts.

To discourage your Ragdoll from scratching your furniture, consider placing scratching posts next to any tempting objects. For example, if your cat has been scratching your sofa, try setting up a scratching post next to the sofa to provide him with a more acceptable option. Location matters to many cats, so you may need to rearrange your furniture to accommodate your cat's scratching needs.

Scratching a new post or pad comes more naturally to some cats, so you may need to introduce your cat to any new purchases. To encourage your cat to interact with a new scratching post, you can try rubbing catnip on it for a few days. You can also include the post in your play sessions by having the cat chase a toy around and onto it. Never force your cat to interact with an object. This can result in a stress response, and your cat may actively avoid using the scratching post or pad.

To further discourage your cat from scratching your furniture, you may need to temporarily make the furniture less desirable. Your local pet store or favorite online retailer will have different types of covers or guards that can be placed over certain areas for protection. These protective surfaces may be slick, spiky, or sticky, which are textures that cats do not like. Double-sided tape can also work.

If you are struggling with your Ragdoll's destructive scratching, consider consulting a feline behaviorist. Declawing is a harmful practice and is not recommended. More information on declawing will be discussed in Chapter 11.

Like scratching, vocalization is a natural behavior in cats, but in some cases, it can become a nuisance. Some breeds, such as Siamese cats, are more vocal than others, but all cats will meow or cry on occasion. If your Ragdoll suddenly becomes more vocal than normal, it could be a sign of pain or discomfort. However, meowing can also be a sign of boredom, and many cats make noise as attention-seeking behavior. If vocalization has become a problem with your Ragdoll, it's important to assess all aspects of your cat's lifestyle and consider whether all of his needs are being met.

Another common bad behavior in cats is urinating or defecating outside of the litter box. This behavior is typically a result of stress but

*Photo Courtesy of
Lindsay Fontaine*

can also be your cat's way of telling you to clean the litter box more frequently. If the box is clean, the behavior could be a result of stressful changes in your cat's life. Moving, construction, new guests or pets, or other changes in the household can sometimes cause a cat to relieve himself around the house. Additionally, urinating outside the litter box can be a sign of urinary issues such as bladder stones or a urinary tract infection. If there are no obvious reasons for your Ragdoll to be going outside of the litter box, it's best to schedule an appointment with your veterinarian as soon as possible.

Many bad behaviors are simply natural reactions to changes in the household, and they may resolve once the change is over or the cat gets used to it. Unwanted behaviors can also be a sign of health issues, so it's important to have your cat examined by your veterinarian to rule out any potential medical causes. In most cases, unwanted or destructive behavior is a result of stress or unmet needs. If there is no medical cause for your Ragdoll's bad behavior, consider consulting a professional feline behaviorist.

CHAPTER 8

All About the Litter Box

Types of Litter Boxes

> "
> *I tell clients to buy a 'simple' litter box for the first couple of months. There are plenty of motorized litter boxes now that may confuse a little kitten. A kitten should just have a small rectangular litter pan. I also ask clients to get traditional clay gravel litter that is non-clumping. Clumping litter is like sand and will stick to anything wet, like the inside of a kitten's eyes. If the kitten's paws are wet, it could end up wearing cement boots!*
>
> MELISSA FIRESTONE
> *Rockstar Ragdolls*
> "

Not all cats prefer the same type of litter box, so you may need to experiment to find which type suits your Ragdoll best. It's generally recommended to give your cat options to see which he prefers best. Most experts recommend having one more litter box than you have cats. For example, if you have two cats, you should have at least three litter boxes for them to choose from. For a single cat, at least two litter boxes are suggested.

One of the most important features of an ideal litter box is size. Ragdolls are large cats, so it's essential that you find a box large enough for your cat to feel comfortable. Some cats will not use a litter box if they

Photo Courtesy of
Sabrina Kapsa - Kingstondolls

feel cramped or if the entry is too cumbersome for their size. Ideally, the box should be large enough for them to move around and dig inside it without stepping out or stepping on any previously used areas.

The height of the walls of your Ragdoll's litter box will depend on his bathroom habits. Cats that tend to spray or those that frequently kick litter out of the box can benefit from higher sides, while cats with more mellow bathroom habits may do fine with a shorter box. It's important to note that young kittens and older cats may have difficulty getting in and out of boxes with high sides, so be sure to take your Ragdoll's mobility into consideration.

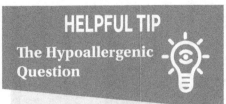

HELPFUL TIP

The Hypoallergenic Question

It's widely believed that Ragdolls are hypoallergenic due to their lack of undercoat and lower-than-average shedding. Unfortunately, this belief is false—there are no true hypoaller-genic cats. In fact, most cat allergies are caused by a protein in a cat's saliva, not its fur. On the bright side, Ragdolls produce less dander than the average cat and may be suitable for people with mild allergies to pet dander.

Some cats prefer to use an uncovered box, while others prefer the privacy offered by a cover. The only way to know what your cat prefers is to set out a covered litter box to see if he will use it. When shopping for covered litter boxes, keep your cat's size in mind. The box itself and the opening should be large enough to accommodate your Ragdoll. Covered litter boxes are generally not recom-mended for cats with asthma or other respiratory issues, as the ammonia and dust from kicking the litter can worsen any existing health problems. However, if your cat insists on using a covered box, be sure to use low-dust litter and clean the box often.

Self-cleaning litter boxes are another option to consider, but they are not always the best option. The boxes themselves can be quite expen-sive, and many require special types of litter, which can also be costly. Despite the convenience of having a box that doesn't need to be scooped daily, these boxes can be an issue for cats with health issues. The daily scooping provides you with an excellent opportunity to monitor your cat's bathroom habits and notice any important changes that could indi-cate the need for a vet visit. If the litter box is cleaning itself, you may not notice these changes right away.

If you have dogs in your home, you may also need to look for a litter box that cannot be accessed by your dog. Depending on your dog's size, a top-entry box may be appropriate. Again, it's important to make sure your cat is comfortable with this mode of entry and that the box is large enough for your Ragdoll to comfortably relieve himself. If your dog is particularly determined to raid the litter box, you may need to consider placing the box on an elevated surface or using a pet gate or other bar-rier. Many pet gates have a smaller opening that will allow a cat to pass but keep out larger pets.

If toilet training your Ragdoll is your goal, you can also find special litter boxes that fit over your toilet seat. These boxes typically come as a set to prepare your cat to use the toilet rather than a litter box. The first step typically involves a tray that fully covers the water in the toilet. As your cat progresses in his training, the hole in the tray becomes larger until your cat is able to use the toilet without any tray. If you choose this option, be sure to only use litters that are safe for flushing. Otherwise, you may have a costly plumbing problem.

Litter Options

There are a number of different types of cat litter on the market, but the most popular is clay litter. Clay was first sold in 1947 and was the first commercially available cat litter. It can be found at nearly any pet store and in grocery and convenience stores as well. It's one of the cheapest options, so it's ideal for cat owners on a budget. Clay litters are available in clumping and non-clumping varieties. Unfortunately, clay litter is also quite heavy and can be dusty and prone to tracking.

Crystal or silica cat litter has risen in popularity in recent years. The crystals are made from quartz sand and are highly absorbent. This litter is not as heavy as clay, so it's a great option for cat owners with weight-lifting restrictions. It's also low dust and low odor. However, crystal litter does not clump, so it's important to mix it daily to encourage proper moisture evaporation. It's also easily tracked out of the box, and some cats may find the texture unpleasant under their paws. Crystal cat litter can also be expensive.

Pelleted cat litter is a great low-dust option and can be made from a variety of materials, including paper, pine wood, and even tofu. Since the pellets are larger, these litters are not prone to tracking. They are also non-toxic and lightweight. Paper is one of the least expensive pelleted litters, and due to the low dust, it is often recommended for cats with health problems or those recovering from surgeries. However, paper is non-clumping and can be difficult to clean. It is not ideal for odor control.

Pine pellets are also an affordable type of litter and have better odor control properties due to their natural pine scent. Pine litter is also non-clumping and can be difficult to clean. Tofu pellets are one of the newest types of litter and are made from all-natural soybean fiber. It's biodegradable and safe for flushing if you are interested in toilet training your Ragdoll. Tofu pellets are also lightweight and clump. However, they can be quite expensive and are vulnerable to spoilage if exposed to moisture in storage.

Other eco-friendly options for litter are walnut and corn litter. These products are made from crumbled walnut shells and corn cobs. They are biodegradable and relatively low dust. Walnut litter is available in clumping and non-clumping varieties, while corn litter is only available in clumping. Both litters can be tracked out of the litter box and are prone to spoilage if stored in moist areas.

When choosing a litter for your Ragdoll, your first priority should be your cat's safety and health. If your cat has any respiratory issues, it's best to choose a low-dust litter. If your Ragdoll has a tendency to eat his litter, you should consider a non-toxic option such as pine pellets or corn crumbles. You should also consider the overall cleanliness of the litter and your cleaning habits. If maintaining a clean litter box and area is difficult for you, it's best to choose a low-tracking litter. Clumping litters are typically easier to clean than non-clumping options, but they can be dangerous if swallowed by the cat. Finally, if you live in a small space, it's recommended to use a litter with odor control. Otherwise, your entire home may have an unpleasant smell each time your Ragdoll uses his box.

Litter Box Training

If you've purchased your Ragdoll from an ethical breeder, it's likely that he has already been introduced to the litter box. However, if your cat has not yet been taught to use a litter box, the process is not difficult. Cats are instinctually clean animals that prefer to bury their waste, so using the litter box comes easily for most.

To introduce your kitten to the litter box, you'll want to set him near or in the box that you have prepared. Some cats will instantly jump out if placed inside and would prefer to enter on their own. While your cat is interacting with the box, just observe quietly and don't distract him. It's

Photo Courtesy of Kaylyne Baker

Photo Courtesy of Susan Brown

recommended to take your kitten to the litter box after all meals and naps to encourage normal bathroom habits. It shouldn't take long for your Ragdoll to figure out what the box is for—but don't expect perfection right away. When you see your cat use the litter box, you can reward him with praise and even treats if you want. Just be sure to wait until he's finished; otherwise, you may interrupt him.

With litter box training, there will always be accidents, so it's important to stay positive and patient with your Ragdoll. Do not punish or scold him, as that will only frighten him rather than teach him the correct behavior. Instead, simply clean up the mess using an enzymatic cleaner to discourage him from returning to that spot.

Common Problems

If your Ragdoll seems to be struggling with litter box training, there could be a number of reasons. If you only have one type of box, your cat may simply not like the size or shape of the box. The smell or texture of the litter could also be an issue. Some cats are more sensitive to these issues than others, so it can be helpful to provide your cat with several options until you determine which one he prefers. The location of the box can also be an issue. Some cats prefer to relieve themselves in private, so if the box is located in a busy area of the house, it may be too stressful for the cat to use it there.

Aside from the litter or box, the cleanliness of the area can also be an issue for some cats. In general, cats prefer using clean boxes. Again, some cats may be pickier than others regarding the cleanliness of their boxes. It's recommended to scoop the box each time your cat defecates and scoop out any urine clumps or wet litter at least once per day or every other day. For picky cats, you may simply need to clean the box more frequently to encourage them to use it.

If you are unable to find a reason for your Ragdoll's resistance to litter training, it's recommended to consult your veterinarian. There may be a medical reason for your cat's bad habits. Cats are not always clear when they do not feel well, so their health problems can sometimes appear to be bad behavior rather than illness.

Toxoplasmosis

Toxoplasmosis is a parasitic infection caused by Toxoplasma gondii. Although it's possible to be infected by eating undercooked meat, you can also contract the parasite from contact with cat feces. Some infected people will not display any symptoms, while others may have symptoms similar to the flu. Young children and people with compromised immune systems are most at risk for serious illness. People who are pregnant are at risk for miscarriage and birth defects, which is why it is commonly advised for pregnant people to avoid cleaning litter boxes. Most toxoplasmosis infections do not require treatment, but people who are pregnant or have weakened immune systems may require medication.

Toxoplasmosis is typically not a concern if your Ragdoll is an indoor-only cat. Cats that are allowed outdoors and can hunt wildlife are more likely to carry the parasites responsible for this disease. If you believe you are at risk for toxoplasmosis, it's recommended to have someone else clean the litter box or to wear gloves and a face mask while handling the litter. Be sure to wash your hands well afterward. During pregnancy, it's also recommended to stay away from stray cats and avoid getting a new cat until after the baby is born. This limits any potential exposure to the parasite.

CHAPTER 9

Grooming Your Ragdoll Cat

Brushing

> "
>
> *Ragdolls have a fine-textured, low-matting coat, but should still be combed at least twice a week—a steel comb works best on the Ragdoll coat. They are a low-shedding breed but tend to shed more seasonally because they get a thicker coat in the fall and winter months. About mid-winter, when the daylight hours start getting longer, the coat will begin to shed, and during this time it's important to groom more often to remove the loose hair. This will help to prevent matting.*
>
> ANN J. LANG
> *Starliterags*
>
> "

Regular brushing helps to remove dirt, skin flakes, and dead hair from your Ragdoll's coat. It also helps to stimulate blood flow and distribute natural oils. Although brushing can benefit Ragdolls of all ages, it's especially important for older cats who may have difficulty grooming themselves. Without regular brushing, the dead hair can create tight tangles called mats, which cannot be brushed out. Mats become tighter with time and moisture and can pull on your cat's skin, causing discomfort and irritation. If your Ragdoll becomes matted, those areas will

Photo Courtesy of
Carole Scott

need to be shaved. Shaving under the mats is the most humane solution, but matting can be prevented entirely with regular brushing sessions.

It's recommended to brush your Ragdoll at least once or twice per week to keep his skin and coat as healthy as possible. Some coats mat more quickly than others, so you may need to adjust your brushing schedule to suit your Ragdoll's specific needs. If you and your cat enjoy the grooming process, you can brush him every day if you choose. Frequent brushing will help to reduce the amount of cat hair left around your home. It will also help to limit the amount of hair ingested by your Ragdoll during self-grooming, which can help with hairballs.

When choosing a brush for your Ragdoll, it's important to use a brush that reaches through the coat to the skin. If you are only able to brush the top layer of coat, it may mat close to the skin and need to be shaved out. Most groomers recommend slicker brushes, which come in a range of sizes, shapes, and tine lengths. A metal comb is helpful as well to check your work and make sure there are no tangles. Both slicker brushes and combs can scratch the skin, however, so it's important to be cautious about the amount of pressure being used. This is especially true for sensitive areas such as the tail, legs, and belly. You may need to

HELPFUL TIP

Do They Mat?

Many longhaired cat owners struggle with their cat's fur matting if tangles are not addressed promptly. The good news about Ragdoll cats is that they are not generally prone to matting, partly due to their lack of undercoat. Despite this benefit, brushing your Ragdoll's coat regularly and providing a well-balanced diet to maintain a healthy and beautiful coat is crucial. In addition, extra grooming during shedding seasons is good practice.

spend more time on sensitive areas and brush using only gentle pressure.

To make sure you remove every tangle from your Ragdoll's coat, it's best to use a method called line brushing. If your cat is used to being brushed, it's helpful to start on a low point on the cat's body, but you may need to start with whatever area your cat is most comfortable with. Using the slicker brush, brush out a small area while holding the coat above the area out of the way with your hand. Once the area is tangle free, use the brush to pull down a small section of the hair you're holding out of the way. Continue to brush your cat one small "line" at a time until you've covered the entire body. After you've finished, you can check your work by running a comb through the coat. If you've missed any tangles, the comb will find them.

Bathing

Cats are clean animals, so they do not typically require frequent baths. In fact, most cats do well without ever getting bathed, as they do a good job keeping their coats clean. However, there are some situations where bathing your Ragdoll may be necessary. Older and overweight cats may not have the mobility needed to keep their coats clean. If your Ragdoll gets into something messy, you may also need to bathe him. Longhaired cats may also need bathing should they accidentally get feces in their hair after using the litter box.

When bathing your Ragdoll, it's important to use a shampoo safe for cats. Cats are very sensitive to certain chemical compounds, so it's crucial that the product is labeled for use on cats. Additionally, some

Photo Courtesy of Carol Letzter

cats have more sensitive skin than others, so you may also want to look for a shampoo with more natural ingredients. Avoid products with long lists of difficult-to- pronounce ingredients, as they may be more likely to cause a reaction.

Before applying shampoo to your Ragdoll's coat, it's best to wet the coat thoroughly with water. The shampoo will spread and lather more effectively on a wet coat. Be sure to avoid spraying your cat's face or ears with the water. As you begin to massage the shampoo into your cat's coat, avoid applying it too close to the cat's face. It's also important to make sure that the shampoo is reaching the cat's skin and that you aren't just washing the top layer of the coat. Many groomers recommend diluting the shampoo with water in a separate bottle or container. This diluted formula is often easier to apply, lather, and rinse than shampoo applied directly to the coat.

Depending on the type of shampoo you use, conditioner may or may not be necessary. If you are using conditioner, be sure to rinse the coat thoroughly before applying. Again, you may want to dilute the product with water, but this will depend on the specific product you're using. It's important to be aware that some conditioners will slow drying time.

The most important part of the bath is the rinse. A good rule of thumb to follow is that once you think you are done rinsing, you should rinse again just to be sure. It's crucial that you remove all product from your Ragdoll's coat. Shampoo or conditioner left in the coat can cause irritation to the skin. Your cat is also at risk of ingesting the product during self-grooming, so make sure to rinse thoroughly.

Despite the stereotype of cats disliking water, many cats enjoy spending time in the water. Bathing a cat that enjoys water will be immensely easier than bathing one who detests it. It's important to be aware that your Ragdoll may react badly to being bathed. If your Ragdoll needs a bath but is too difficult for you to handle, it's recommended to seek the help of a professional groomer. Not all groomers are willing to work with cats, so you may need to do some research to find the right professional for the job.

Drying

After your Ragdoll's bath, be sure to dry him as thoroughly as possible with a soft towel. Longhaired breeds can take quite a while to air dry, and a wet coat can chill your cat, so try to shorten the drying time as much as you can. Many cats will not tolerate rough handling while towel drying, so try to absorb the moisture with gentle pats and smooth motions. Your cat will likely attempt to dry his coat himself, so don't be surprised if he begins frantically licking himself.

If your cat will tolerate it, you may also want to use a hair dryer. If you are using a human hair dryer on your cat, be sure to keep it a safe distance away from your cat's skin. Many dryers get hot quickly and can burn your cat if you aren't careful. By keeping one hand on your Ragdoll as you dry, you can help fluff the coat and monitor heat levels.

Trimming or Clipping

Despite their long coat, Ragdolls do not generally need to be clipped or trimmed. Although it may seem heavy during the warmer months, their coat actually helps to insulate their bodies from not only the cold but heat as well. As long as you are able to keep the coat brushed out and free of mats and tangles, there should be no reason for your Ragdoll to need a haircut.

However, a haircut may be the best option for your Ragdoll under certain circumstances. If he is heavily matted, clipping him may be the most humane option. Older cats that struggle with self-grooming and do not tolerate brushing well may also benefit from clipping. It's important to note that if you do choose to clip your Ragdoll, you will need to protect him from the sun and extreme temperatures. A clipped coat exposes the cat's skin and puts him at risk for sunburn.

In most cases, it's recommended to take your Ragdoll to a professional groomer if you choose to trim his coat. Many cats can be difficult to handle for grooming, and cat skin is incredibly thin and easy to cut. It takes a certain amount of skill to be able to safely groom a cat without injury or stress to the animal or groomer.

Unlike dogs that have specific styles for each breed, there is no specific grooming style for Ragdoll cats. You may choose to have your cat shaved evenly all over his body, but most people choose to leave the head, legs, and tail. Some owners prefer a lion cut, which leaves the cat with a lion-like mane and short body. You may choose to have the entire tail left long or just the end. The legs may also be left long, or they may be trimmed partially to resemble boots. Discuss with your groomer to determine what style is best for your Ragdoll.

Perhaps your Ragdoll just has a few small mats on his body and does not require a full-body clip. You may choose to have just the mats shaved out while preserving the rest of the coat. This is a valid option, though it may look a little silly while the coat grows out. However, you should always prioritize your cat's comfort over his appearance. It is not recommended to remove mats yourself with scissors. As stated previously, it's incredibly easy to accidentally cut a cat's thin skin, especially with scissors. If you are going to remove a mat, it's best to use clippers or have a professional groomer handle the matter.

If you choose to trim your Ragdoll's coat, you should be aware that you will still need to keep up on brushing as the coat grows out to prevent mats. You will also need to brush any areas, such as the tail, mane, and legs, that are left longer. Shaving your cat will not stop him from shedding. Your cat will still shed the same amount he normally does, but the hairs will simply be shorter.

Nail Care

> 66
>
> *When sitting with your kitten, play with its feet a lot—this includes pushing the claws out. This will make it much easier when the time comes to clip the kitten's nails! If the kitten or cat is not thrilled with nail clipping, do one foot at a time and give it a break in between.*
>
> KEN STAPLES
> *Kasseldolls*
>
> 99

If you have issues with your Ragdoll's scratching, you may want to trim his nails regularly. Unlike a haircut, nail trims can be done by a professional groomer, but many owners can handle it themselves with a little practice and proper handling. However, if you would rather not trim your cat's nails yourself, it's typically quite inexpensive to have your vet or groomer do it.

There are typically two types of nail trimmers used for cats: guillotine style and scissor style. Guillotine-style nail clippers are not recommended, as they can crush the nail if they are not sharp enough. Scissor-style trimmers result in a cleaner cut and safer experience.

Some cats will tolerate nail trims without a struggle, but others may require a bit of restraint. To prevent injury to yourself or your cat, it's recommended to wrap your cat with a towel or blanket, exposing only one paw at a time. Choose a quiet room to work in to minimize stress and distraction.

When you're ready to trim your Ragdoll's nails, gently press the toe to expose the nail. At the base of the nail, you will see a pink area called the quick. The quick is the nail's blood supply, and it will bleed profusely if cut. It's also very painful for the cat to have the quick cut, so it's important to trim carefully to avoid this area. It's recommended to leave about one-eighth of an inch in front of the quick. Use your clippers to quickly snip off the sharp end of the nail. Try not to hesitate while trimming, as your cat may react to the pressure on his nail and pull back. Repeat this process for each of his other nails, and don't forget the dewclaws on the inside of each foot.

If you do accidentally cut the quick, it can be helpful to have styptic powder or gel on hand to stop the bleeding. Cornstarch can also work, but it is not as effective. Simply pat a small amount of styptic powder or cornstarch on the tip of the nail and wait a few moments for the bleeding to stop. Try not to let your cat run off immediately after application, as he may lick off the powder and bleed on your furniture or flooring.

Nail caps are another solution for scratching that can be applied at home or by your vet or groomer. If you aren't familiar with nail caps, they are little plastic covers that attach to your cat's nails with a cat-safe adhesive. They last for four to six weeks and do not cause any pain or discomfort. Your Ragdoll will still be able to comfortably retract his nails with caps on. They come in a range of colors and sizes to suit every cat and owner. You may also choose between applying caps to all four paws or just the front. Back caps may be helpful if your cat tends to scratch your furniture when jumping off or if he has a habit of scratching himself excessively.

Although caps are painless, your Ragdoll may act strangely the first few days after application. This behavior is normal, as he is simply reacting to something new. After a few days of fussing, his behavior should return to normal. Most cats get used to nail caps quickly and handle subsequent applications without issue.

To safely apply nail caps, you must first trim your Ragdoll's nails. Application may depend on the specific brand of nail cap you've purchased, but in general, it is a simple process. In most cases, you will put a small amount of adhesive inside the cap before sliding it over your cat's nail. If the adhesive oozes from the sides after application, you'll need to use less on the next one. It should take only a few moments for the glue to dry enough to stay on the nail.

The nail care options here should not be used on Ragdolls that spend any amount of time outdoors. A cat's claws are one of its main methods of defense, and you may be putting your outdoor cat's life at risk if you trim his nails or use nail caps. Capping and trimming nails should only be done on indoor-only cats.

Ear and Eye Care

Most cats do not need assistance in keeping their ears and eyes clean and healthy. However, it is important to monitor your Ragdoll so that you can take action if you notice anything unusual. It's a good habit to casually check your cat's eyes and ears each day as you give him affection. Be sure to look down into the ear canal and examine the outer ear structures.

If you notice any redness, swelling, or discharge, call your vet as soon as possible. Serious ear and eye issues will need to be addressed with medication. For example, your vet may want to swab the ear and examine it under a microscope to determine whether the problem is a yeast infection or mites. These problems require different medications, so it's best not to try to diagnose the problem yourself.

Photo Courtesy of Stormi Nell - FamilytimeRags

If your cat's ears or eyes are simply dirty, you can address this problem at home. Look for ear and eye cleaning products labeled for use with cats. You can then use a cotton ball with eye wash to gently wipe away any dirt at the corners of the eye. With ear cleaner, it's important to use only a cotton ball and your fingers, not a cotton swab. Cotton swabs can reach further into the ear and can potentially cause injury. Gently wipe the ear out and follow with a dry cotton ball.

Finding a Groomer

When searching for a professional groomer, it's important to find a groomer that is familiar with cats. Not all groomers are willing or able to work with cats, but there are some groomers who choose to work with cats exclusively. The more experience your groomer has with cats, the safer your Ragdoll will be. Some groomers have mobile businesses, which allow them to come to your location to groom your cat. Others have stationary shops that you will need to transport your cat to. Be aware that mobile groomers are often more expensive. The cost of having your Ragdoll groomed will vary by location as well as the specific services you request.

If you have friends or family with cats that get groomed regularly, you may want to ask them for a recommendation. Your veterinarian may also be able to recommend a groomer that works with cats.

If your Ragdoll is difficult or dangerous to groom safely, your groomer may recommend having your cat groomed at a veterinary clinic. Many vet clinics have groomers in-house, but the benefit of this arrangement is that your cat can be safely sedated. Groomers that work with veterinary staff are typically knowledgeable in safely handling and grooming sedated cats. Additionally, if your cat has any issues with sedation, veterinary staff are nearby to provide care if necessary.

CHAPTER 10

Feeding Your Ragdoll

Benefits of Quality Nutrition

A nutritious diet is an essential part of your Ragdoll's overall health and well-being. Nutrient imbalances can cause serious problems for cats of any age, but growing kittens are especially at risk for developmental issues. Many of the effects of nutritional imbalances are not immediately apparent, so serious damage can be done before the signs of malnourishment appear. Some of the effects of a nutritional deficiency can be repaired, but many are permanent, so it's crucial that you feed your Ragdoll a balanced, high-quality diet.

In addition to balanced nutrients, portion size is another crucial aspect of a proper diet. Obesity is one of the most common health problems facing domestic cats of all breeds. That excess weight puts unnecessary strain on your Ragdoll's joints, which can result in limited mobility and a shorter life span. Weight management will be discussed later in the chapter, but it's important to remember that portion size is just as important to consider as the food itself.

HELPFUL TIP
Hairball Help

Nutrition plays a crucial role in preventing hairballs in your Ragdoll. Experts suggest a high-quality diet with plenty of fiber to help keep things moving in your cat's digestive tract. Nutrient-rich food will also prevent your Ragdoll from losing excessive hair, thus preventing more fur in its digestive tract after grooming. Hairballs are often expected and seasonal but can sometimes lead to problems. Symptoms of a hairball problem include bloating, unproductive hacking, lethargy, and lack of appetite.

It should be noted that cats are obligate carnivores and must consume meat to survive. Cats do not generally tolerate a vegetarian or vegan diet. Some nutrients can be gained from plant material, but most of the nutrients required by your cat are found in animal products. Additionally, cats' digestive systems have not evolved to properly digest large amounts of carbohydrates.

If you have any concerns about the ingredients in your cat's food, it's best to discuss the matter with your veterinarian or a feline nutritionist. If you are interested in finding a veterinary nutritionist to work with, the American College of Veterinary Nutrition (ACVN) has a list of board-certified nutritionists on its website.

Commercial Diets

The most common type of commercial diet fed by cat owners is kibble. Kibble is convenient to purchase, store, and feed and can be found in nearly all areas of the country. It's also one of the least expensive cat foods, though there is some range due to quality and ingredients. Kibble is available in a wide range of formulas, which makes it ideal for almost all cats. Different proteins are available to suit cats with sensitivities or preferences as well. Additionally, there are different formulas for cats of different ages and those with specific health issues.

Another popular choice for cat owners is canned food. Canned food is just as easy to find and store as kibble, and many cats find it to be more palatable. It's an ideal choice for finicky felines who don't like the crunch of kibble. Canned food also contains more moisture, so it's a great choice for cats who struggle to stay hydrated. As with kibble, canned food comes in a variety of formulas to suit the different needs of individual cats. One of the downsides of canned food is that it tends to stick to the teeth more than kibble, so there is more of a buildup of plaque and tartar. Cats on wet food diets may require more frequent dental cleanings.

Fresh-cooked cat food is becoming a popular diet for cats of all breeds and ages. It's typically found in the refrigerated section of your local pet or grocery store. There are even companies that send a fresh-cooked diet for your cat straight to your door. This type of food is usually packaged in a roll or patty and can be cut into proper portion sizes. It must be stored

in the refrigerator between uses and can go bad if left beyond its expiration date. Fresh food diets are typically more expensive than kibble or canned food, but many picky cats prefer it if their owners can afford it.

Commercially available raw diets are another option that is rising in popularity. Many cat owners are looking for a more natural and species-appropriate diet for their cats, and raw diets have filled that niche. They can be found in the frozen section of your local pet supply retailer and can be quite expensive. Most raw foods contain a balanced combination of muscle meat, bone, organ, and some fruit and vegetables. These foods also come in a variety of protein options and contain few, if any, grains or artificial ingredients. Raw food must be stored in the freezer until it's ready to be used, but most cats prefer it to be thawed to room temperature. As with all raw meat, there is some risk of pathogens, so proper hygiene and cleaning protocols must be followed, especially if anyone in the household is immunocompromised.

Homemade Diets

If you are having trouble finding the right diet for your Ragdoll, you may want to consider making his food yourself. However, it's important to note that commercial cat food is required by law to meet certain nutritional standards, so it will be your responsibility to make sure your homemade cat food maintains a correct nutritional balance. It's highly recommended to work with a veterinary nutritionist to formulate a high-quality, balanced homemade diet for your cat. As previously stated, the ACVN has a published list of veterinary nutritionists on its website. Though the organization is American, they list nutritionists from around the world.

There are typically two types of homemade feline diets: cooked and raw. Raw diets are meant to simulate the type of diet a cat would have in the wild. The specific ratio of muscle, bone, and organs reflects the approximate ratio found in prey animals. It should be noted that raw bones are safe for cats to eat, while cooked bones are not. Cooked bones have a tendency to splinter, which can potentially cause injury. If you are uncomfortable giving your cat bones, you may want to consider using a meat grinder or a powdered calcium supplement. Again, it's best to seek advice from a nutritionist if you are swapping out ingredients.

Cooked diets are popular with cat owners who want a healthier diet for their cats but are not comfortable feeding a fully raw diet. The ingredients in a cooked diet are typically quite similar to those in a raw diet but are baked or boiled before being fed. Many cooked diets are also higher in carbohydrates and plant matter.

When making your Ragdoll's food at home, it's crucial that you follow safe handling guidelines for raw meat. Remember, cats' digestive systems are meant to handle small amounts of common pathogens such as salmonella. Humans can get very sick if they consume anything contaminated. While handling raw meat for your cat's food, you need to be extremely careful about cleaning your prep area afterward. If your cat tends to carry his food away from his bowl, you may also need to restrict his space during mealtime. If he carries his food around the house, he could potentially be spreading pathogens throughout your home. Carpet and fabric on furniture can be particularly difficult to sanitize, so try to feed your cat on an easy-to-clean surface such as a tile or linoleum floor or a silicone mat. You may also consider wiping down your cat's face and paws afterward if you are concerned about bacteria.

Ingredients to Avoid

> *It's important to keep Ragdolls on a diet with high-quality foods. READ FOOD LABELS! Seriously, read the labels on the food you are giving your baby. Don't use something with a lot of fillers and ingredients you can't even pronounce, and don't buy food just because it's a cheap brand. This doesn't mean you have to use the most expensive brand either—use a mid-priced brand that seems healthy. Also, feed wet food at least once a day—that can help to prevent crystals and urinary problems with your cat.*
>
> CONNIE STALLINGS
> *Ragdolls Whiskers*

Not all human foods are safe for cats to consume, so it's important to be aware of what ingredients you can and cannot include in your Ragdoll's diet. Toxic foods can cause serious health problems and can be fatal in large quantities. If you suspect your Ragdoll has eaten something toxic, call your veterinarian as soon as possible.

Common human foods that are toxic to cats include:

- Onions
- Garlic
- Chocolate
- Caffeine
- Grapes & raisins
- Meat with seasoning or spices

You should also be careful not to feed your Ragdoll dog food, as it contains a different nutrient profile. Specifically, it lacks a nutrient called taurine. Dogs are able to produce their own taurine, so they do not require it in their diets. Cats' bodies cannot produce taurine, so they must consume it in their food. Without it, they can develop heart disease and vision or dental issues.

Although some foods, such as fat and organ meat, are safe for cats to consume, they can cause digestive upset in large amounts. Fat and organ meat are very rich and can cause vomiting and diarrhea if the cat eats too much. If you are using these ingredients in your cat's homemade diet, it's important to limit the amount to what is recommended by your nutritionist or veterinarian.

Weight Management

> *Please do not feed your Ragdoll all dry food! Having a diet based on wet food is so important—you show me a cat that eats all dry food, and nine times out of ten, I will show you a chubby kitty. Obesity is not cute. It is dangerous for all animals and causes cancer, heart disease, and even arthritis. Love your cat? Then give it a proper diet and exercise.*
>
> BETTE WILLETTE
> *Willetteragdol*

Photo Courtesy of Julie Stocker

According to the Association for Pet Obesity Prevention in 2018, it was found that around 50% of cats in the United States were overweight or obese. Many of the owners of those cats were unable to recognize that their cats were above a healthy weight range. Although some owners may recognize that their cats are heavier than they should be, many don't fully realize the detrimental effects of excess weight.

It's important to note that there is no specific weight range recommended for Ragdoll cats. The healthiest weight for an individual cat is determined by its size and build and will vary even among littermates. Rather than looking at a number, you should determine your cat's healthiest weight by body condition. At an ideal weight, your cat should have a visible waist when viewed from above. From the side, the stomach should tuck up slightly behind the ribs. The ribs should not be visible

Photo Courtesy of Sharon Sisitzky

but should be easily felt when palpated. If you are not sure if your cat is at a healthy weight, consult your veterinarian.

As mentioned earlier in the chapter, one of the most important aspects of weight management is portion control. In addition to your cat's daily meals, you will also need to consider the calories in any treats or snacks your cat may enjoy throughout his day. If your Ragdoll is overweight, you will need to reduce his meal size as well as his snacks and treats. Some cat food brands offer a low-calorie option, which can help to cut back on calories without leaving your cat hungry. If you are feeding your Ragdoll a commercial diet, most brands provide feeding guidelines on the packaging. These guidelines are an estimate that can be adjusted to your cat's specific needs. Your veterinarian or veterinary nutritionist may also be able to give you more exact feeding recommendations.

The other key to proper weight management is physical exercise. The more active your Ragdoll is each day, the more he can eat while maintaining a healthy weight. If your cat needs to lose weight, you will need to encourage him to be more active each day while also cutting calories. Just be sure to start slow, as he will need to gain fitness. Just a few minutes of play each day can add up, so don't worry about encouraging long play sessions just yet. The fitter your cat gets, the more willing he will be to participate in physical activities.

CHAPTER 11

Your Ragdoll's Health Care

Choosing a Vet

I f you have other pets in your home, you may already have a preferred veterinarian. If you don't, you'll need to do some research to find the right vet for your new Ragdoll cat. It may take some time to find the right fit, but when you do, you'll feel comfortable knowing that your Ragdoll is in the right hands.

If your breeder is local, he or she may be able to provide a recommendation. One of the benefits of working with your breeder's vet is that they will be familiar with the breed and will likely have provided your cat care since he was born. If your Ragdoll came from a rescue organization, they might also be able to recommend a local vet. Cat-owning friends and family may also be a great resource to consult in your search for a new vet.

For further help, consult an online directory such as those on the American Veterinary Medical Association (AVMA), American Association of Feline Practitioners (AAFP), or American Holistic Veterinary Medical Association (AHVMA) websites. These directories are often searchable by species and treatment type.

Many small animal vets provide care for both cats and dogs, but if your Ragdoll has issues being around dogs, you may want to find a cat-only veterinary clinic. Feline-specific veterinary clinics are not available in all areas, but they are a great place to find staff familiar with handling nervous cats.

Photo Courtesy of
Stephanie Wineland

When searching for a vet, you should also consider your normal schedule. If you would prefer not to miss work for a vet appointment, look for clinics open evenings or weekends. Some clinics are only open during normal business hours from Monday through Friday, but some may be open 24 hours a day. Twenty-four-hour clinics are ideal for after-hours emergency care, so even if you don't intend to use them for routine care, it can be helpful to have their information on hand. Some veterinary clinics may also offer special low-cost events for spaying and neutering or vaccinations, which can be helpful if you are on a tight budget.

Regular Vet Visits

It may seem silly to take your Ragdoll to the vet if there's nothing wrong, but routine vet visits are key to a healthy cat. Depending on your Ragdoll's overall health, your vet may recommend routine examinations every 6 to 12 months. Older cats or those with chronic health conditions will likely need to see the vet more often. Even if your cat is healthy, it's recommended to see your vet at least once per year.

Routine vet visits are a great way to monitor your cat's overall health. When you spend so much time with your Ragdoll, it can sometimes be difficult to see small changes in his body condition or health. For example, you may not immediately notice that your cat has been gaining weight over the past few months. Since your vet will have a record of your Ragdoll's condition at his last vet visit, he or she will be able to tell you about any small changes you may not have noticed. Additionally, if you have any concerns about your Ragdoll's health or behavior, these regular visits give you the opportunity to discuss them.

Feline dental care is often overlooked, but regular vet visits will help you keep track of your Ragdoll's dental health. During the physical exam, your vet will look at your cat's mouth to make sure the teeth are clean and healthy. If there is a buildup of plaque and tartar, your vet may recommend a dental cleaning. The frequency at which your Ragdoll will need dental cleanings will depend on his diet and overall health. Your vet may also be able to make recommendations to improve your cat's dental health, such as changes in diet or at-home dental care techniques.

Regular vet visits also ensure that your Ragdoll stays up to date on vaccinations and deworming. Some vaccines

HISTORICAL FACT

Frank and Louie

In 1999, a Ragdoll cat named Frank and Louie was born with a rare condition called diprosopia. Cats with this disorder, also called Janus cats, are born with two faces. Frank and Louie's original owner brought this cat to a clinic to be euthanized, but a sympathetic nurse brought the cat home with her instead. Frank and Louie died at the age of 15 and was featured as the longest-surviving Janus cat in the Guinness Book of World Records in 2006.

must be updated every year, while others will need to be updated every few years. Your vet will be able to recommend the best vaccination schedule for your Ragdoll based on his age, overall health, and lifestyle. If your Ragdoll spends any time outdoors, keeping him up to date on vaccinations and deworming is essential, as he is exposed to more parasites and pathogens than an inside-only cat.

Photo Courtesy of
Anwyn Statnick

Microchipping

If you've purchased your Ragdoll from an ethical breeder, the cat may already have had a microchip implanted. If not, you will need to discuss microchipping with your vet on your first visit. Even if you do not allow your Ragdoll outdoors, it's still important to microchip him. Accidents can happen, and someday your cat may slip out an open door or window. If he is not wearing a collar with an identification tag, it may be next to impossible to be reunited with him. Microchipping ensures that your cat can be identified regardless of whether he is wearing a collar and tag.

Microchips are small devices that are similar in size to a grain of rice. They are inserted beneath the skin with a needle, typically just above the shoulder blades. When scanned with a microchip reader, the microchip can be identified with a specific number connected to your contact information. Although there may be some minor discomfort during insertion, microchips are not painful for the cat. There are few side effects, though some microchips may migrate to other parts of the body. For this reason, many shelters and vet clinics scan the animal's whole body when checking for a microchip. If your cat's microchip does migrate, your vet may recommend inserting a new one just to be safe.

Microchipping is typically not expensive, though you may need to pay your vet for implantation and then pay a separate fee to the microchip company for registration. The specific cost will depend on the brand of microchip and the area in which you live. You may also be able to find low-cost microchipping clinics in your area.

Once your Ragdoll has been microchipped, you will need to remember to update your contact information with the microchip company if you change addresses or phone numbers. If you do not keep the information up to date, it will be difficult to be reunited with your lost cat.

Vaccinations

Vaccines can be divided into two categories: core vaccines and non-core vaccines. Core vaccines are those recommended or required for all cats. Many core vaccines are combined into a single syringe to eliminate the need for multiple injections. However, rabies vaccines are always given separately. Non-core vaccines are recommended more selectively based on the cat's location and lifestyle.

The five core vaccines recommended by the American Association of Feline Practitioners (AAFP) are the following:

- Feline panleukopenia virus (FPV)
- Feline viral rhinotracheitis (FHV-1)
- Feline caliciviruses (FCV)
- Feline leukemia virus (FeLV)
- Rabies virus

FPV causes severe and often fatal stomach and intestinal infections, also known as gastroenteritis. It is highly contagious to other cats, so vaccination is crucial.

FHV-1 and FCV cause upper respiratory infections. Cats may be infected by FHV-1 or FCV separately, but they may also occur together. Although the disease is typically not severe enough to be fatal for adult cats, it can cause long-term health problems.

FeLV is a widespread and highly contagious virus that can cause immune system damage and tumors. Symptoms of FeLV often do not appear immediately, so your vet may ask to perform a blood test on your Ragdoll before vaccination.

Rabies is one of the most serious viruses as it can be transferred to other animals as well as humans. Once an animal shows the neurological symptoms of rabies, the disease is almost always fatal.

Non-core vaccines that may also be recommended include the following:

- *Chlamydophila felis*
- *Bordetella bronchiseptica*
- *Feline Infectious peritonitis (FIP)*

Chlamydophila felis is a virus responsible for feline chlamydiosis or chlamydial conjunctivitis. This disease is not common in all areas, but it is frequently found in feral cat colonies. It causes painful swelling of the membranes around the eyes as well as upper respiratory infections. In female cats, it can also cause infertility.

Bordetella is a disease that results in an upper respiratory infection. It's highly contagious and can spread quickly in a multi-cat household or cattery environment. Though rarely fatal, it can take several weeks for symptoms to resolve with veterinary care.

Your Ragdoll likely received his first vaccine between six and eight weeks of age. After that, booster shots are recommended every four weeks until the age of 16 to 20 weeks. As an adult, your Ragdoll will need booster doses on occasion, but the frequency will vary by location and lifestyle. Low-risk adult cats may need core vaccine boosters every three years, while higher-risk cats may need them annually.

HEALTH ALERT!
Recognizing Parasite Problems

Gastrointestinal parasites are common in cats and can be tricky to spot without testing. Symptoms of parasite infections can include vomiting, diarrhea, bloating, coughing, and a dull coat. Regular screening for parasites should be done by a veterinarian who can prescribe the necessary medication to rid your cat of destructive parasites. Experts suggest testing your Ragdoll for parasites annually, at a minimum. Common parasites affecting Ragdolls include roundworms, hookworms, tapeworms, and whipworms.

It's important to note that although vaccine reactions are rare, they do happen on occasion. Some cats may seem a little lethargic or have less of an appetite than normal, but this should resolve after 24–48 hours. More serious reactions can include vomiting, diarrhea, and difficulty breathing. If your cat displays any of these symptoms, contact your veterinarian immediately.

Parasite Prevention

If your Ragdoll is an indoor-only cat, parasite prevention is relatively easy, but if your cat spends any time outdoors, you will need to maintain a regular routine. External parasites can easily be seen with the naked eye, but internal parasites require testing by your veterinarian. At the very least, annual fecal exams are recommended to test for internal parasites. Annual blood tests for heartworms are not currently recommended for cats as they are for dogs, but your vet may recommend a monthly preventative, depending on your area.

Common intestinal worms found in cats include roundworms, hookworms, and tapeworms. Protozoa, such as giardia, toxoplasma, and isospora, can also be found in cats, depending on where you live. Internal parasites are typically acquired by ingesting infected food, water, feces, or soil. Fleas and ticks are the most common external parasites, though the species of tick can vary by location. Fleas and ticks are generally picked up as the cat walks through infested areas such as tall grass or brush.

Symptoms of intestinal parasites include lethargy, sudden weight loss, diarrhea, and excessive gas. Cats with a heavy parasitic load may have a distended belly with an otherwise malnourished body condition. Cats infected with heartworm may display symptoms such as coughing, rapid breathing, weight loss, and vomiting.

Treatment for intestinal parasites typically includes oral medication, though treatment time varies by parasite species. Some parasites can be treated with a single dose of medication, while others may require several weeks of treatment. Heartworm treatment is more serious and can take several months. During treatment, physical activity must be limited to prevent the blockage of major blood vessels.

Spaying and Neutering

As a responsible pet owner, you should be prepared to spay or neuter your Ragdoll at an appropriate age. Spaying is the surgical procedure that removes your female cat's ovaries and uterus, while neutering is performed on male cats to remove the testicles. There are numerous benefits to spaying and neutering your Ragdoll unless you intend to show your cat in championship classes or start a breeding program. If you are interested in showing your Ragdoll, you can still compete in premiership or household pet classes if the animal has been spayed or neutered. Showing your Ragdoll will be discussed in more detail in Chapter 13.

*Photo Courtesy of
Bette Willette*

One of the most significant benefits of spaying and neutering is the effect it has on many bad behaviors. Hormones are often to blame for urine marking, roaming, and aggression, but surgical alteration typically reduces or eliminates these behaviors. Spaying and neutering also prevent your cat from falling ill with uterine infections, prostate problems, and some types of cancer. Additionally, these procedures help prevent unwanted litters that can contribute to overpopulation in shelters and rescue organizations.

Most veterinarians recommend spaying or neutering your cat by around seven months of age. As your Ragdoll reaches sexual maturity, he may begin displaying problem behaviors, so many vets recommend altering before it becomes an issue. However, your vet will be able to evaluate your Ragdoll's overall health and determine the best age for spaying or neutering.

With the advances in modern veterinary medicine, these procedures are incredibly safe, and complications are rare. As long as at-home care instructions are carefully followed, your Ragdoll should recover with little downtime. If you have any concerns about anesthesia or the procedure itself, be sure to talk to your veterinarian beforehand.

If you are interested in breeding your Ragdoll, it's recommended you work with your Ragdoll's breeder so that you can follow ethical cat breeding guidelines. Having a mentor can help ensure that your breeding program contributes to the improvement of the Ragdoll breed. Breeding is not without risk, so working with an experienced breeder will also ensure your Ragdoll receives the best care possible before and after any kittens are born.

Declawing

Declawing is essentially the surgical amputation of the cat's claws and the toe bones to which they are attached. It's most frequently performed on the front paws only, but sometimes all four paws are declawed. Declawing is generally performed on young cats due to the lower risk of complications and is sometimes done at the same time as spaying or neutering.

In an attempt to prevent their cat from scratching the people and objects in their homes, some owners opt to have their cats declawed. However, declawing has become a topic of debate. Many European countries have outlawed declawing as they consider it to be a cruel and unnecessary procedure. Since scratching is a normal behavior for cats, many believe that declawing causes emotional stress and may affect the animal's ability to balance and climb. Some studies also show an increase in problem behaviors, such as biting and eliminating outside the litter box following declawing. Furthermore, declawing removes one of the cat's natural forms of defense, which can put the cat at risk of injury or death if faced with a serious threat.

Although declawing is not illegal in much of the United States, fewer vets are willing to perform the procedure. If you are considering declawing your Ragdoll, it's recommended to discuss the matter with your veterinarian. He or she may be able to offer more humane alternatives, such as regular nail trims or nail caps. You may also want to contact a professional feline behaviorist if your Ragdoll's scratching behavior is beyond that of a normal cat.

Common Genetic Conditions

Although Ragdoll cats are relatively healthy, there are a few genetic conditions to be aware of. An effort is currently being made by ethical Ragdoll breeders to eliminate these conditions from the gene pool by health testing cats before breeding. Two of the most common genetic conditions in Ragdoll cats are hypertrophic cardiomyopathy (HCM) and polycystic kidney disease (PKD).

HCM is the most common cardiac disease in cats of all breeds, but it occurs in the Ragdoll breed at a higher-than-average rate. This disease causes a thickening of the heart wall, which reduces the volume of blood in the heart as well as the heart's ability to adequately pump blood throughout the body. With poor circulation, the cat is then at risk of developing blood clots.

Symptoms of HCM include shortness of breath or difficulty breathing, open-mouth breathing, lethargy, appetite loss, and weight loss. Sadly, this disease cannot be cured, but symptoms may be treated with close monitoring, medication, and oxygen therapy. Unfortunately, once clinical signs of the disease are present, little can be done to prevent the progression of hypertrophic cardiomyopathy.

Polycystic kidney disease is a genetic condition that causes cysts to form within the kidneys. Typically, the cysts are present from birth but grow larger over time. Eventually, they will disrupt the kidney's function and cause the organ to fail. The age at which symptoms develop varies, but many cats will not show signs until around seven years. However, some cats will experience kidney failure at a much younger age, depending on the growth of the cysts.

Symptoms of PKD include lethargy, weight loss, decrease in appetite, excessive water intake and urination, nausea, and vomiting. PKD does not require any specific treatment, and affected cats are generally treated the same as those with chronic kidney disease. Fluid therapy, special diets, and medication are used to treat the symptoms of kidney failure. However, it should be noted that not all affected cats will display symptoms of the disease, and those with fewer or slower-growing cysts may live full lives without issue.

Photo Courtesy of Bonnie Gleason

PKD is commonly found in Persian cats but may also be found in Ragdolls with Persian or Exotic Shorthair heritage. The gene that causes PKD is autosomal dominant, which means that all cats with the abnormal gene will be affected. Even if a cat with the affected gene does not show clinical signs of PKD, he or she may still pass the disease on to future kittens. For this reason, genetic testing is crucial in preventing the disease from being passed on to the next generation of Ragdolls.

Pet Insurance

With the rising cost of veterinary care, many cat owners are exploring options to help reduce the cost of keeping their pets happy and healthy. Pet insurance policies are becoming more popular as more companies offer a range of policies with premium prices and coverage levels to suit all budgets. Many policies only cover emergency veterinary care, but some may also include preventive care. Not all policies are equal, however, so it's important to do some research to find the right policy for your Ragdoll. It's also important to note that senior cats and those with preexisting conditions may cost more to insure or may be denied coverage entirely.

Most insurance companies also have waiting periods, and many have different waiting periods for different conditions. For example, some policies have waiting periods of 7 to 10 days for accidental injuries and around 14 days for illnesses. Orthopedic issues often have a longer waiting period of up to 30 days or more. This means that if your Ragdoll gets injured or falls ill during the waiting period, his treatment will not be covered by insurance.

If you are considering pet insurance, it's best to purchase a policy sooner rather than later. Healthy, young cats are generally less expensive to insure, and you can be sure that you are covered if any health problems arise.

Over the lifetime of your Ragdoll, monthly premiums can add up. Some owners instead choose to put their money into a separate account each month to save for any future vet bills. Since many cats do not develop serious or costly health conditions until they are older, the savings can be enough to cover treatment without having to worry about negotiating with an insurance company. Pet insurance isn't right for every owner, so it's important to consider all of your options before signing anything.

CHAPTER 12

Traveling with Your Ragdoll

> *Many cats prefer a closed-off, dark carrier, but Ragdolls are curious, so offer them a carrier with 'windows.' Or use a dog kennel that is open so the Ragdoll can look out and see its person—visual information is valuable to a Ragdoll. They make great travelers; they sleep well under airplane seats; they are happy in an RV looking out the window at wildlife ... they even like walks in strollers!*
>
> ELIZABETH BOATWRIGHT
> *Masterpiece Ragdolls*

Car Travel

Although cats aren't often thought of as travel companions, many cats enjoy accompanying their owners on road trips and vacations. The key to successful car travel with your Ragdoll is preparation. So if you know you will be traveling with your cat, it's best to begin preparing as soon as possible.

The first step in travel preparation is to acclimate your Ragdoll to his carrier. You can start by having the carrier open in the house and making it as inviting as possible. Cozy bedding and plenty of treats will help encourage your Ragdoll to spend time in the carrier. Once your cat is comfortable entering and exiting the carrier, you can close the door

Photo Courtesy of Deona Good

and walk around the room. Be sure to reward your Ragdoll with treats and plenty of verbal praise and petting afterward. As your cat gets used to being carried, you can walk out to the car and back. If your Ragdoll is comfortable leaving the house, try setting the carrier in the car and starting it up. If all goes well, you can progress to a quick trip around the block. Again, be sure to provide plenty of rewards for calm behavior.

It's never recommended to travel with a cat unrestrained in the car. An unrestrained cat is a danger to you and other drivers. If the cat becomes frightened or nervous, he could jump on you and potentially distract you from the road. Additionally, if you were to be involved in an accident, your cat could easily escape out a broken window and run away or into traffic. It's much safer to acclimate your cat to a carrier.

Depending on how far you will be traveling, you may want to set up a small litter box in the car. If your Ragdoll's carrier isn't big enough to accommodate a small box, you can set one up on the car floor or in the cargo area. If the litter box is outside of the carrier, you'll want to make sure all doors and windows are closed before allowing your Ragdoll out for a bathroom break. Don't forget to offer your cat a drink of water each time you take a break; otherwise, he may become dehydrated. If the drive is not long, you may want to wait until you get to your destination to set up a litter box. While traveling, it's recommended to use the same litter as you do at home to avoid disrupting your cat's normal bathroom routine.

Photo Courtesy of Audrey Bodnar

It's recommended to line the carrier with a disposable puppy pad to absorb moisture. Some cats can get carsick on their first few trips in a vehicle, and absorbent pads can help with clean-up. You may also want to bring a few extras, just in case, as well as a plastic bag to store any soiled pads until you are able to dispose of them.

In addition to a box and litter, it's important to remember to bring all of your cat's necessary supplies on your car trip. To avoid digestive upset, you'll want to continue feeding your cat the same food you give him at home. Some cats can be picky about water, so you may want to consider bringing a bottle of water from home. Additionally, you will want to bring a blanket or cat bed from home so your Ragdoll has something with a familiar scent to sleep on. Don't forget the toys and grooming supplies if you plan on being gone for several days or more.

If you are traveling with your cat out of state or out of the country, it's important to check on the legal requirements of your destination. You should always travel with vaccination records, but depending on your destination, you may also need to get a health certificate from your vet before travel.

> ❝
> *Most Ragdolls are very easy travelers. For long trips, there are pop-up cages that will hold a litter box as well as a bed. It is best to keep food and water on hand, but not in the crate, to avoid spilling. Make sure to offer food and water at every stop.*
>
> MINDY FERREIRA
> *BellaPalazzo*
> ❞

Air Travel

If you plan on traveling with your Ragdoll by plane, it's important to prepare far in advance. You will first need to find a carrier for your cat that is airline approved. Not all airlines have the same requirements for carrier dimensions, so you may need to plan your trip before purchasing the carrier. For a large cat such as a Ragdoll, a soft-sided carrier is best if you are traveling with your cat in-cabin. If you will be traveling with your Ragdoll in cargo, a hard-sided carrier is recommended.

In addition to acclimating your cat to his carrier, you will need to book his travel with the airline as early as possible. Remember, you will need to pay an extra fee for your cat in addition to the cost of your own ticket. If you are traveling roundtrip, you will need to pay the fee each way. Additionally, if you are switching airlines during a layover, you may also need to pay a separate fee for each flight. Many flights have restrictions on the number of pets allowed, so it's best to book as soon as you can. If you want your cat to fly with you in-cabin, you will also need to choose your seat accordingly, as pets are not allowed for passengers traveling in an exit row or against a bulkhead.

You will also need to get your travel documents in order, as the airlines may ask you for health certificates and vaccination records. Not all airlines will, but you should be prepared anyway. This is especially important if you plan on traveling internationally, as you will be asked for documents when passing through customs.

If you are traveling with your Ragdoll in-cabin, you will need to take him out of his carrier to go through security. His carrier will need to pass through the X-ray screening

HELPFUL TIP

Silent Sufferers

This breed has a reputation for being particularly non-vocal, so much so that the cats often fail to alert their humans when something is amiss. Understanding cat body language is especially important for Ragdoll owners, who may get no other indication of how their cats are feeling. There are many variations to cat body language, but your Ragdoll's tail will generally be your best indicator. An upright tail indicates extreme happiness, a relaxed tail shows contentment, and a low, swishing tail indicates agitation.

FAMOUS RAGDOLL

The Algonquin Cat

A luxury hotel near Times Square in New York has a resident Ragdoll that has gained internet fame. Hamlet, the Algonquin's "most important resident," is named after one of the hotel's residents, John Barrymore, who was famous for his role as Hamlet in 1922. To observe this Ragdoll's life of luxury, you can follow him on Instagram or Twitter at @thealgonquincat.

device, which means you will need to carry your cat through the human screening device. It's recommended to outfit your Ragdoll with a well-fitting harness and leash to make sure he can't run off if he escapes from your arms.

Many veterinarians do not recommend sedation for travel, but if you think your Ragdoll will be overly stressed during the flight, you should discuss it with your vet. There may be options to consider other than sedation, including pheromone sprays or collars and natural supplements. Getting your cat used to his carrier and being carried while inside will go a long way toward reducing stress on travel day.

As with car travel, you should consider lining your Ragdoll's carrier with a disposable pad to aid in clean-up should he get sick or have an accident. You may also want to bring a few extras, just in case. Additionally, you'll want to bring your cat's normal food and any medications he may need. It can be difficult to carry litter and a litter box during air travel, but you will need to remember to purchase any necessary supplies when you reach your destination.

Cat-Friendly Accommodations

When planning a trip with your Ragdoll, it's important to look for cat-friendly accommodations. Not all accommodations allow pets, and many that do charge an extra fee for housing an animal. However, it's not usually difficult to find somewhere to stay with your feline companion.

There are a number of hotel chains that allow pets. Again, some may charge an extra fee while others may not. You may also want to explore other options, including bed and breakfasts and short-term rentals. When searching for accommodations, it's also important to keep your Ragdoll's comfort in mind. A busy hotel with a lot of noise may not be ideal for a nervous cat, so a rented house or condo may be a better option.

No matter where you choose to stay, it's essential that you are a courteous guest. Some people traveling with pets allow their animals to be messy and disruptive, which can cause the hotel or homeowner to reject pet owners in the future. Try to keep your Ragdoll entertained so that he does not disrupt other guests, and be sure to clean up any messes. Of course, travel often does not go as planned, so try to be patient with your host if any problems do arise. Additionally, be patient with your Ragdoll, as it can take a few days to settle into a new environment, especially if he is new to traveling.

Leaving Your Cat Behind

Not all cats are meant to be travel companions, so if you need to leave your Ragdoll behind, you'll want to make sure he's taken care of. There are many options to consider, including pet sitters and boarding facilities. Even some veterinary clinics offer boarding services. If you're traveling on a budget, you may want to consider asking a friend or family to take care of your Ragdoll while you're gone. The cost of pet sitters and boarding facilities varies by location and services offered, so you may want to call several places to see what works with your ideal budget.

If you are interested in leaving your Ragdoll at a boarding facility, be aware that they will require proof of vaccinations. Some may also ask that your cat is dewormed or treated for fleas and ticks before drop-off. If the boarding facility is connected to a veterinary clinic, they may be able to take care of everything there. Otherwise, you'll need to plan in advance to make sure you have enough time to schedule an appointment with your vet.

Most boarding facilities are happy to give you a tour of the area your cat would be staying in. If they are hesitant to have owners see their space, it could be a red flag, and you may need to look elsewhere. Many boarding facilities have different size spaces available to suit your cat's needs, though they will vary in price accordingly. A single-cat condo

Photo Courtesy of Vickie Hatfield

should ideally have elevated areas and hiding places to give your Ragdoll a sense of comfort. If you have multiple cats and would like to have them stay together, many facilities offer oversize kitty condos or even whole rooms to accommodate a big feline family.

If your Ragdoll is nervous around dogs, be sure to look for a facility that keeps cats in a separate area away from the dog kennels. If the spaces are separated by only a wall, your cat may still be able to hear the barking, which can result in a stressful stay. Some areas offer feline-only boarding services, which may be a better option for nervous cats.

In addition to basic care, which likely includes daily feeding, watering, and litter box cleaning, you will want to ask what additional services are offered. Some facilities include a certain amount of play and cuddle time each day, while others may charge extra. You may also be able to purchase extra time if your Ragdoll needs a bit more daily attention. If your cat takes medication regularly, you may need to pay an additional fee to have it administered, especially if it's an injectable medication.

To make your Ragdoll's stay at the boarding facility as comfortable as possible, it's recommended to bring his regular food, litter, and bedding. Many boarding facilities offer food and litter, but your cat may have a difficult time adjusting to an entirely new environment. A few familiar things will help minimize stress while you're away.

If you'd prefer for your Ragdoll to stay at home while you travel, consider hiring an in-home pet sitter. Many pet sitters offer both drop-in and overnight services. Drop-in visits mean that the pet sitter will stop in one or more times per day to feed and water your cat, change his litter, and spend a little time playing or snuggling. An overnight sitter will stay in your home through the night to make sure your Ragdoll gets all the attention he needs. Typically, overnight services are more expensive than drop-ins, but it will depend on your area and the number of drop-ins requested.

In addition to caring for your cat, many pet sitters offer basic home care services such as collecting your mail each day and watering your plants. If you plan on traveling for a long period of time, an in-home sitter can help keep your house in good condition until you return. Additionally, it will deter any potential thieves that may be targeting empty houses in your neighborhood.

If you would like to hire a pet sitter, be sure to look for a sitter that is insured and has references. Ideally, you should set up a meeting with the sitter so that you can get to know them and introduce them to your Ragdoll. This person will be staying in your home and taking care of your beloved companion, so it's important to trust them. If anything about the person makes you uncomfortable, it's best to continue your search. During the initial meeting, you will want to ask about the sitter's basic charges and what that entails. If you are requesting additional services, this is a great time to discuss any additional charges.

No matter where you choose to leave your Ragdoll, it's important to leave behind emergency contact information should anything unfortunate occur. You should give the boarding facility or pet sitter the best way to contact you in an emergency, whether it is by phone or email. You may also want to leave the contact information of a close friend who may be available in person if needed. It's also recommended to leave the contact information for your veterinarian, but you may also request that your cat be taken to the nearest clinic if an emergency should occur.

Remember, if you've done your research, you're leaving your Ragdoll in good hands. Stressing about leaving him behind will only serve to make him more stressed, so try not to worry. The more confident you are about leaving your Ragdoll with his temporary caretakers, the more comfortable he will be during his time with them.

CHAPTER 13

Into the World of Showing

All About Cat Shows

As the owner of a purebred cat, you may be interested in getting involved in the world of cat shows. Since Ragdolls are recognized by nearly all cat registries, you should be able to participate in most shows. However, your Ragdoll will need to be registered with the organization you intend to show with. For example, if your Ragdoll is CFA registered, you can easily attend a CFA show, but you will need to register him with TICA if you intend to show him at a TICA-sanctioned cat show.

There are several organizations in the United States that hold cat shows. A few of the most popular include the following:

- Cat Fanciers' Association (CFA)
- The International Cat Association (TICA)
- Cat Fanciers' Federation (CFF)
- American Cat Fanciers' Association (ACFA)

Cat shows are typically held on the weekends, as most participants, as well as the judges and volunteers, work during the week. At a show, there are generally several rings running concurrently. A different judge presides independently over each ring, essentially resulting in a number of separate competitions running at once. Although cats may compete in multiple rings, they may not receive the same awards due to the differing opinions of the judges.

Each purebred cat entered in the show is evaluated by the judge against the breed's written standard. The standard describes the ideal

Photo Courtesy of
Ebah Wolf

specimen for the breed, and the judge must use it to determine the quality of the cat. Although the standard remains the same for each judge, they may have different interpretations, which is why the results of each ring may differ.

Cat shows are typically classified as either all-breed or specialty. All-breed shows allow all cats to compete for the various awards, while specialty shows only allow cats of similar coat length or type. Additionally, there are separate competitions for pedigreed cats and household pets. As the name implies, pedigreed cat competitions are for purebred cats only, while any cat may compete in a household pet competition, regardless of its pedigree status. Pedigreed cats who do not meet their breed standard may also compete in household pet competitions, though they must be spayed or neutered if they are over the age of eight months.

No cats, regardless of pedigree status or age, are allowed to compete if they have been declawed. Many organizations require competitors to clip their cats' claws prior to showing to ensure the safety of the judge while handling.

In the pedigreed cat competition, the cats are further divided into kitten, championship, or premiership classes. Kitten classes are for

HELPFUL TIP

What Are Pointed Cats?

Ragdolls are considered "pointed cats," meaning their colors darken as they age. All Ragdoll kittens are born white but will start to gain color by eight to 10 weeks old. Ragdoll coloring, as recognized by the RFC, includes Seal, Blue, Chocolate, Lilac, Red, Cream, Tortie, and Torbie. Most of these colorings can be point, bi-color, or mitted.

purebred cats between the ages of four and eight months. Once the cats reach eight months of age, they are required to enter either championship or premier classes. Championship classes are intended for cats destined for a breeding program, so all competing cats must be intact. Premiership classes are for cats that have been spayed or neutered. It's common for championship cats to compete in premiership after they are done breeding and have been spayed or neutered.

Whether a cat is showing in kitten, championship, or premiership, it will initially compete against cats of the same color, breed, and gender. The winner of each gender will then go on to compete against the opposite gender but still within the same breed and color category. Once the Best of Color winner has been chosen, that cat will compete against other colors of the same breed. Best of Breed winners of all breeds then compete against each other for the prestigious title of Best in Show.

Some cat shows also offer agility competitions. They are similar to dog agility competitions, where a cat must complete an obstacle course in an enclosed area. Each run is timed, and cats receive points based on the obstacles successfully completed. Bonus points are awarded if the cat completes the course under the maximum allowed time. In agility, all cats compete against each other regardless of their pedigree status. A grand champion purebred could win just as easily as a household pet.

In agility, the cats are lured through a series of obstacles using a toy. The handler is not allowed to touch the cat but may use the toy to convince the cat to navigate each obstacle. The obstacles found on the course include jumps, tunnels, weave poles, and more. Not all shows offer agility classes, but they are a fun and exciting opportunity to compete outside of the conformation ring.

Ragdoll Breed Standards

Breed standards are one of the most important aspects of producing a breed with consistent type. As breeders seek to produce a cat that closely resembles the ideal Ragdoll, they are ensuring the preservation of the breed. Without a standard, breeders would be breeding cats with different appearances, and the result would not be the Ragdoll as we know it. This is the reason that breeders take their cats to shows to be evaluated by judges. It can be difficult for people to see the flaws in their beloved cats, so they need outside opinions. Cat show judges are able to give knowledgeable and qualified opinions on how closely individual cats adhere to their breed standards. Breeders can then make educated decisions on which cats they should breed to produce the next generation of Ragdoll cats.

It's important to note that not all Ragdolls will resemble the breed standard. In a litter of Ragdoll kittens, there may be one or two that

Photo Courtesy of
Mindy Ferreira - Bellapalazzo Ragdolls

Photo Courtesy of Diane Moore

do well in the show ring, while the others may be better suited as pets. Though they may be wonderful companions, the kittens that do not closely resemble the breed standard should not be bred, as they may produce kittens that are even further from the ideal Ragdoll cat.

According to the breed standard, the Ragdoll can be described as a well-balanced cat that should not have any extreme features. They are medium- to large-sized and moderately longhaired. The overall appearance of the breed should give the impression of subdued power and graceful movement.

The head of the Ragdoll is proportionately large, with a broad wedge shape and a gently rounded muzzle. Male cats typically have larger jowls, especially if they have not been neutered. The Ragdoll's eyes are a signature characteristic. They are large, oval-shaped, and moderately slanted. Regardless of coat color, the eyes are always a vivid blue. The ears should be medium in size and wide set.

The Ragdoll's body should be large and long with heavy boning. The overall shape is rectangular, with a full chest and hindquarters. Some Ragdolls may have a moderate stomach pad on their lower abdomen. Male Ragdolls are typically larger and more masculine in appearance than females. The legs should be heavily boned and moderately long. The Ragdoll's hind legs are longer than the front, and they should have shorter fur on the front legs as well. The tail should be long with a full plume of fur.

The Ragdoll's moderately long coat is another signature characteristic of the breed. The coat should have abundant guard hairs and minimal undercoat. There should be a ruff of fur around the neck. The hair should be short on the face, longer on the ruff, and slightly shorter on the shoulder blades. Ragdolls should have full, feathery britches on their hind end. It's important to note that although this describes the ideal Ragdoll coat, some variations are permitted due to hormonal and seasonal changes.

Traits penalized in the show ring include a thick undercoat or a coat that stands off the body. Small, round eyes or eyes that are too light or dark of a shade of blue should also be faulted. Ragdolls should not have a cobby body, short legs, or a short tail. Disqualifying traits include any coat color other than the colors listed here and eyes that are any color other than blue. Ragdolls are also disqualified if they have crossed eyes, extra toes, or a directional kink in the tail. As discussed in Chapter One, acceptable coat patterns include bi-color, colorpoint, mitted, and van. These patterns are allowed in a variety of coat colors, including chocolate, seal, lilac, blue, lynx, red, cream, and tortie.

Getting Started in Cat Shows

If you've purchased your Ragdoll from a local breeder, he or she may be able to help you get involved in cat shows. If your cat's breeder is not local, you will need to do a little research on your own. It's highly recommended that you attend a few cat shows as a spectator before you enter your Ragdoll for the first time. Spectating will help you better understand how cat shows work and what will be expected of you and your Ragdoll.

Many show organizations, such as the CFA, have volunteers who act as ambassadors. These people are a great source of information if you have questions about showing. Additionally, most exhibitors are happy to chat with spectators so long as they are not on their way to the ring. Cat shows are busy environments, so you should always ask an exhibitor if they have time to talk to you. Even if they are busy at the moment, many people will welcome your questions at a less hectic time.

As a show spectator, it's important to understand that you may not touch anyone's cats without permission. A lot of time and effort goes into grooming show cats, and exhibitors can be very particular about who handles their cats. You may ask permission to touch the cats—but don't be offended if you are told no. The same rule should apply to taking photos of the cats. Many exhibitors are fine with spectators taking photos, but you should always ask permission first.

When you are ready to enter your first cat show, you will need to fill out an official show entry form. Depending on the show, the form may be available online, as a PDF, or on paper. You will need to fill out the form completely, entering information such as your Ragdoll's registered name, registration number, sex, breed, and color. The form may also ask for the names of your cat's sire, dam, and breeder unless you are entering your cat as a household pet. Additionally, you will need to provide your contact information, including your phone number, address, and email. You will then need to specify which class you are entering your Ragdoll in. At the end of the form, there may be several items listed that you may request if available, though some may come with an extra charge. This can include extra cage space or grooming space as well as cage space in certain areas of the show grounds. Finally, you will need to pay your entry fees. The amount of fees will depend on what classes you enter your Ragdoll in,

Photo Courtesy of
Sabrina Kapsa - Kingstondolls

Photo Courtesy of Angela Jackson

as well as any additional requests you have made.

As your show date approaches, you will need to gather the necessary supplies. Most shows provide exhibitors with a cage for their cat and at least one chair unless you have requested something different on your entry form. It's important to be aware of the size of cage you will be using at the show, as you may want to buy "show curtains" to give your cat a sense of safety and privacy. Although show curtains can be purchased for a number of cage sizes, you can also use a flat sheet. Many exhibitors choose to color-coordinate all of their show equipment. For example, you may choose show curtains that will match your cat's bed and the lining of the cage. If you want to start simple, you can always check out the vendors at the show to see if they have something for sale that you would like for next time.

You should also bring a litter box, litter, food and water bowls, cat food, and fans if it will be warm. You can also bring cleaning supplies, towels, and plastic bags to take care of messes or accidents. Of course, you will also need to bring any grooming supplies you may need for last-minute touch-ups. You should also consider bringing snacks and drinks for yourself and any human companions, as well as quiet entertainment, such as books or playing cards. It's also recommended to have a bit of cash on hand for food and beverages. Plus, you never know when you might find something you can't live without at one of the vendor booths.

On the day of the show, it's recommended to show up at least an hour before the judging begins to make sure you have enough time to set up and get comfortable. You will need to check in with show officials, find your assigned cage, and get it ready for your cat. At check-in, you will receive a show catalog, which will list the information for all cats entered in the show. Your cat will be assigned an entry number, so be sure to find your cat in the catalog and locate his or her number. This number will be used to identify your cat for the duration of the show, so it's important to remember it. The catalog will also contain the judging schedule so you will know what order the classes will take place and in which show rings. The only time listed will be the time when judging begins, so you will need to pay attention to the ring and compare it to the judging schedule. That way, you are ready when your group is called to the show ring.

When you take your cat to the show ring, the cage you place your Ragdoll in will have his entry number on it. Place the cat in the cage, make sure the door is latched securely, and find a comfortable place to sit or stand in the audience area. Unlike dog shows, cat owners do not take an active part in handling their animals in the show ring. All handling will be done by the judge. Once the judge has finished, the ring clerk will announce that the cats may go. You can then collect your cat and any ribbons that have been hung on the cage. If your Ragdoll has done well, you may be called back to the ring later in the day for additional judging.

If the show is both Saturday and Sunday, you may leave your cage set up Saturday night so that it is ready for your cat on Sunday morning. After the show is over on Sunday, you will need to collect your belongings, clean up your area, and head home to celebrate your experience. Remember, if you have any questions during your time at the show, don't be afraid to ask other exhibitors, show volunteers, or even judges if they are not busy. Even if they don't know the answer to your question, they will be able to direct you to the right person.

CHAPTER 14

Your Aging Ragdoll Cat

> *When your Ragdoll reaches an advanced age, it will slow down considerably. I'd suggest switching to a window-height cat tree as the cat will no longer be as agile as it once was; if you place the tree by the window, your cat can enjoy watching the sunrises and sunsets. You may want to keep other pets away at this time—at this age, cats prefer solitude and a lot of sleep. This will be the time to show your cat love and appreciation for all its years of devotion.*
>
> JOSE ANTONIO CARMONA JR.
> *Purrfect Ragdolls Delaware*

Common Signs of Aging

Not all senior cats experience the same signs of aging, nor do they experience changes at the same age. Some cats may reach their late teens without issue, while others may develop health problems at an earlier age. In general, cats are considered elderly around the ages of 11 to 14 years. Cats over the age of 15 years are sometimes referred to as super seniors due to their advanced age.

One of the most common signs of aging in cats is a loss of energy. Senior cats tend to be less active than their younger counterparts. They may be less playful than they once were and spend more time napping.

This change in energy often contributes to a change in weight as well. Arthritis can also reduce an older cat's mobility. You may notice your Ragdoll having difficulty jumping onto high surfaces, or he may be less willing to climb up to his usual perch.

As they age, some cats may experience a decline in hearing or vision. Your Ragdoll may not respond as quickly when you call him, or he may startle easily when woken from a nap. Most cats adapt well to these changes, but you may need to adjust how you approach your Ragdoll to avoid startling him.

One of the most difficult signs of aging is cognitive decline. Your Ragdoll may begin to appear confused from time to time, or he may have difficulty navigating certain spaces. Occasional confusion is relatively normal, but if you notice it frequently, your Ragdoll may be developing more serious cognitive issues, and a vet visit may be in order.

Some cats also develop changes in behavior as they age. Not all behavioral changes are a concern, but some can be a sign of more serious health problems. For instance, some cats become clingier as they age and enjoy spending more time cuddling in their golden years. Others may begin avoiding human interaction, which can be a sign of pain or illness. If you have any questions about your Ragdoll's behavior, be sure to ask your veterinarian.

Basic Senior Cat Care

> 66
>
> *Ragdolls can live a long, healthy life if taken care of properly. Regular vet checks and healthy foods can help ensure the longest life. If you purchased your Ragdoll from a breeder that does all required veterinary and genetic testing, ask to see those test results so you'll be aware of any potential genetic issues early on.*
>
> WILLIAM MICHAEL VAUGHN
> *Exclusive Ragdolls*
>
> 99

Photo Courtesy of Anwyn Statnick

When caring for your senior Ragdoll, it's important to prioritize his comfort. This may mean you need to rearrange furniture or adjust certain spaces to better suit his needs. Many older cats enjoy resting in warm places, so you can try placing your Ragdoll's favorite bed in a sunny window or near a heat source. Just be sure the area doesn't get too hot. If your senior cat has mobility issues, you may need to place his bed on a lower surface or provide him with stairs or a ramp to reach his favorite spot. Sometimes it only takes a small change to make your aging Ragdoll a bit more comfortable.

It's also recommended to provide your senior cat with more litter box options. If you own a multilevel home, it's best to place at least one litter box per floor. Many older cats struggle with stairs as they begin experiencing the effects of age, and it can be difficult for them to make it to the litter box in time. Additionally, you may need to replace your Ragdoll's litter boxes if they have high sides or are otherwise difficult to enter. Senior cats do best with larger boxes with low sides.

As your Ragdoll gets older, you may also want to consider more frequent check-ups at the vet. Many vets recommend check-ups as frequently as every six months or so for healthy senior cats. If your Ragdoll has any health problems, you may need to schedule visits more often. At an advanced age, health can decline quickly, and more frequent visits give your vet more opportunities to catch and address any problems as soon as possible.

Older cats also have different grooming needs than when they were younger. Some seniors may stop grooming themselves entirely or in certain areas due to discomfort or reduced mobility. This can quickly lead to a matted coat, so you may need to brush your Ragdoll more often as he gets older. You will also need to be gentler in your handling while grooming. Your Ragdoll may not be as tolerant of the brush tugging on his hair as he once was. Instead, it's better to brush him more often to prevent tangles.

Some senior cats may also experience a loss of vision or hearing, so you may need to adjust your home accordingly. If your cat has trouble seeing at night, you may want to consider placing nightlights near his litter box, food, and water, and any difficult-to-navigate areas such as stairs. You will also need to be more careful about how you approach your Ragdoll to avoid startling him. Try not to approach him from behind, especially if he's napping. Gentle words at a volume that he can hear will also warn him of your approach.

Illness and Injury Prevention

> Check your cat's weight and document it regularly—that can be the first sign that something is wrong. Check its teeth frequently as well. If your cat's grooming habits change, that can be a sign of something wrong and is a good reason to get a health check-up. The coat can either become oily or very dry in some cases when there is a health issue.
>
> STORMI NELL
> *Familytime Rags*

Your main priority in caring for your aging Ragdoll is to keep him as happy and healthy as possible in his final years. In order to prevent illness and injury, you may need to make a few changes in your home. Many older cats do not fully recognize their limitations, especially as they

*Photo Courtesy of
Sherry Goeben*

first begin experiencing signs of aging. As a result, they may attempt physical feats that they are no longer capable of. While you cannot prevent every illness or injury, you can take steps to keep your Ragdoll as safe and healthy as possible.

As previously mentioned, you may need to provide easier access to your Ragdoll's favorite spaces. This may mean lower-

FUN FACT

Slow Growers

Ragdolls reach their full size later than many other cats. These cats are considered adults once they reach 12 months but will continue through growth spurts for another three years. Generally, male Ragdoll cats can reach 15 to 20 pounds or more, and females are often 10 to 15 pounds.

ing surfaces or providing ramps or stairs. Depending on your Ragdoll's preferred litter box type, you may also need to invest in a box with lower sides so that he can climb in and out more easily. By making your Ragdoll's favorite spaces more accessible, you can help reduce the risk of injury. Senior cats with limited mobility and strength may still try to climb or jump onto high surfaces, which can result in injury if they miss and fall.

If you live in a home with tile or hardwood floors, you may also need to provide your Ragdoll with traction on slippery surfaces. As he ages, your Ragdoll may have a more difficult time keeping his feet under him on certain surfaces. Rugs or mats can provide traction and prevent any injuries. If you are using pet stairs or a ramp to give your Ragdoll access to high surfaces, be sure that they have carpet, turf, or another nonslip surface.

As mentioned earlier in the chapter, it's recommended to schedule more frequent check-ups at the vet to monitor your senior Ragdoll's health more closely. Depending on your cat's condition, your vet may also recommend regular blood work to gain a better perspective on your Ragdoll's overall health. Some medications can also affect liver function, so regular bloodwork may be necessary, and medication can then be adjusted accordingly. Additionally, if you notice any changes in your aging Ragdoll's health or behavior, it's recommended to visit the vet as soon as possible. Remember, some conditions can progress quickly, so the sooner you seek treatment, the better.

Senior Cat Nutrition

> *I've found that my older cats drink more water if they have a cat fountain. Choose a ceramic or stainless-steel fountain—NOT plastic. Drinking lots of water will help keep cats healthy as they age. Have their teeth checked too—a dental cleaning can significantly lengthen the life span of your kitty.*
>
> ANN J. LANG
> *Starliterags*

Not all cats experience age the same way, especially when it comes to their nutrition. Some seniors may lose weight, while others may gain weight or remain the same. It's important to adjust your Ragdoll's diet to suit his changing body and help him maintain a healthy weight.

Adjusting your Ragdoll's meal sizes can help keep him at a healthy weight. Free feeding is not recommended as it can make it difficult to monitor your cat's daily food intake. Instead, set out a single portion of food two or more times per day. If your Ragdoll does not finish his meal each time, then you know that you can reduce the amount you set

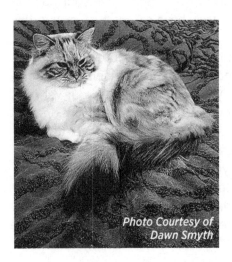

Photo Courtesy of
Dawn Smyth

out. However, if he is not finishing meals and is losing weight or is too thin already, you will likely need to change his food rather than portion size. If your cat should lose a bit of weight, reducing portion sizes and increasing physical activity is best. However, be sure to increase exercise slowly, as older cats will need more time to build fitness.

In addition to changing portion sizes, many senior Ragdolls require a new diet entirely. Finicky eaters may need something more enticing, while overweight cats may need a food lower in calories. If your Ragdoll has developed any health problems, your vet may also prescribe a veterinary diet as a treatment. Many senior cats do better with wet food in their diet. Canned food is typically easier to eat and contains more moisture, which can aid in hydration. As a reminder, more information on different types of diets can be found in Chapter 10.

Senior cat foods are specifically formulated to meet the needs of aging cats. Unlike foods that are formulated for all life stages, senior diets contain ingredients that can help aging cats stay fit and healthy. For example, many

Photo Courtesy of Allison Romano

senior cat foods contain enhanced antioxidant levels to provide extra support to their immune systems, which may be declining with age. The ingredients in senior diets are also typically more digestible and have optimized calorie levels to help cats maintain an ideal body condition. Many senior foods also contain ingredients such as glucosamine and chondroitin to support joint health. If you are unsure which type of food would best benefit your senior Ragdoll, ask your veterinarian for advice.

CHAPTER 15

When It's Time to Say Goodbye

When to Say Goodbye

Unfortunately, there will come a day when you will need to say good-bye to your Ragdoll. You know your cat better than anyone, so you will have to be the one to make this crucial decision. It may be difficult, but it's important to remember that a peaceful and pain-free death is one of the greatest gifts you can give to your pet.

Seeing past the sorrow and grief can be difficult for many people, and it can be hard to decide whether your cat is ready for his journey over the Rainbow Bridge. One way to determine if it's time to say goodbye to your beloved Ragdoll is to use the H5M2 quality of life scale. The scale was developed by veterinary oncologist Dr. Alice Villalobos. For many owners, it can be a helpful and objective method of evaluating your cat's quality of life. The scale uses seven categories, which are each given scores of zero to 10 points. If your Ragdoll's overall score is below 35, it's likely that his quality of life has diminished, and humane euthanasia may be recommended. A total of 70 is a perfect score, representing an ideal quality of life.

The categories of the H5M2 scale are:

- **Hurt** – Consider how much pain your Ragdoll is in on a daily basis. Is his pain under control with medication? Can he breathe without distress?
- **Hunger** – Evaluate your Ragdoll's appetite and his ability to consume adequate nutrition. Is he able to safely and comfortably

maintain a healthy body condition? Can he eat on his own, or must he be hand-fed or fed through a feeding tube?

- **Hydration** – Does your cat drink enough water on his own, or does he require subcutaneous fluids to maintain an appropriate level of hydration? Using your cat's current weight, calculate 10 ml per pound to determine an appropriate amount of water intake per day.
- **Hygiene** – Consider your Ragdoll's overall hygiene. Can his fur and skin be kept clean and free from feces and other bodily fluids? Can he move or be moved enough to prevent the development of sores?
- **Happiness** – Does your cat still enjoy his favorite activities? Is he responsive to his surroundings? Does he engage in play or seek affection from his family members, or does he appear to be depressed and uninterested?
- **Mobility** – Is your Ragdoll able to move freely on his own to meet his own needs? Is he at risk of stumbling or falling while walking?
- **More good days than bad** – Compare your Ragdoll's number of good days to bad. It can be helpful to keep a calendar or journal to keep track.

If your Ragdoll's overall score is above 35, you may consider continuing with hospice or palliative care. If your cat is suffering from a chronic illness, you may need to periodically evaluate his quality of life. It can be difficult, but it's important to be prepared with a plan for when his score deteriorates further. As your Ragdoll's sole caregiver, it's your responsibility to protect him from the pain and frustration he may be feeling in his final days. Ideally, your cat's passing should be as peaceful and painless as possible.

HELPFUL TIP

How Long Do They Live?

The average life span of a Ragdoll cat is 12 to 15 years, but many Ragdoll owners report their cats living to be 19 or older. One of the leading causes of death for this breed is hypertrophic cardiomyopathy (HCM). Cats affected by this disease are at heightened risk for sudden cardiac arrest and death. Recent research has shown that genetic markers for this disease exist and can be screened for by Ragdoll breeders. Unfortunately, there is currently no cure or prevention available for HCM.

The Euthanasia Process

To prevent unnecessary suffering in an animal's final days, most owners opt for humane euthanasia, which is always performed by a licensed veterinarian. Some states may allow a veterinary technician to perform the procedure so long as the veterinarian is present to supervise. Euthanasia involves injecting a lethal dose of sodium pentobarbital directly into the bloodstream. It does not induce any stress, anxiety, or pain. However, many vets will administer a mild sedative prior to the injection to further relax the animal, especially if the pet is nervous about being handled by strangers.

Your veterinarian will likely prepare your Ragdoll for euthanasia by placing an IV catheter. The catheter makes it easier for the vet to inject both the sedative and euthanasia solution. Once the catheter is in place, the sedative can be given. The sedative acts to relax your cat so that he will allow the veterinary staff to monitor and handle him without stress or discomfort. Most intravenous sedatives act quickly, so your Ragdoll should relax after just a few minutes. Once the sedative has taken effect, the euthanasia solution will be administered.

Sodium pentobarbital acts quickly to slow and eventually stop the heart. Again, there is no discomfort; the pet quickly loses consciousness and drifts away peacefully and painlessly. The entire process rarely lasts longer than a minute. After the injection is administered, your vet will use a stethoscope to monitor your Ragdoll's heart rate and verify the moment that the heart and breathing stop.

Once the heart has stopped, your vet will likely give you a few moments alone with your Ragdoll to grieve. Your veterinary staff understands how difficult this time is, and they are typically willing to be as accommodating as necessary to make sure you get to properly say goodbye to your beloved feline.

Final Arrangements

When the time comes to say goodbye to your beloved Ragdoll, you will likely be struggling with grief and sorrow. It can be difficult to make decisions in this state of mind, so it's helpful to make a plan for your cat's final arrangements in advance. Unfortunately, you won't always know when the time will come, but it's a good idea to have a plan in mind should something happen.

Euthanasia can typically be performed at a veterinary clinic or in your home. If your vet does not offer both, you may need to find a vet that offers the service you prefer. Some owners feel more comfortable saying goodbye to their companion in the comfort of their own homes, while others prefer to distance the painful memory from their home. There is no right choice, and you should do what works best for your Ragdoll and your family.

As you make final arrangements, consider whether you want to be present during your Ragdoll's final moments. Again, this is a personal choice. If you choose not to stay, know that your veterinary team will be there to provide your beloved pet with the love and comfort he needs in his last moments. You will also be able to spend time alone with your Ragdoll after the procedure if you need time to grieve. Veterinarians and staff understand that this is an emotionally difficult time and are typically able to accommodate owners' wishes. You may also be

Photo Courtesy of Julie Stocker

able to pay in advance so that you won't need to worry about it afterward. The clinic may also have an alternate exit for you to use so that you won't need to leave through a busy waiting room.

You will also need to make a decision about your Ragdoll's remains. If you choose to arrange your companion's burial or cremation yourself, you may request to take the remains with you. Otherwise, your veterinary clinic will be able to make those arrangements for you. If you choose cremation, you will also have the choice of whether you want the ashes to be returned to you.

Grieving Your Loss

The loss of your beloved Ragdoll can leave you with feelings of sorrow, frustration, and emptiness. The silence of your cat's absence in your home can be especially upsetting. Grief is not something you "get over" but rather something you grow with. Remember, there is no set time period for grieving, and it can take time to adapt to living with loss.

In a joint study done in 2018 by the Schools of Veterinary Medicine

Photo Courtesy of Diane Moore

of the University of California and University College Dublin, researchers found that about 25% of pet owners felt intense grief for three to 12 months, 50% for 12 to 19 months, and 25% for 12 to 24 months. Don't feel that you have to rush through your feelings or shift your mood overnight. Take as long as you need to experience your feelings.

As you mourn the loss of your feline companion, try to remember all the good times you had together. That unique bond you had is something to be grateful for. For some people, it can be helpful to write down their memories or their feelings in a journal. You can also put together a photo album of your favorite memories. You can have friends or family send you their favorite pictures of your Ragdoll to help you remember your favorite moments together.

Photo Courtesy of Sara Coxon-Fortin

You may want to consider preparing a memorial for your Ragdoll. There are many options for this, depending on how you would like to remember your beloved cat. You can do something as simple as planting a tree or decorating a stone in your yard or garden. You may also consider volunteering at or donating to a rescue organization in your Ragdoll's memory. Try to choose something that you feel connected to based on the relationship you had with your cat.

If you've had your Ragdoll's ashes returned to you, you can also seek out the talents of artists that are able to turn the ashes into art or jewelry. Ashes can be incorporated into many mediums, including glass, ceramics, and paint. Some artists are able to incorporate pet hair into their art as well. There are also many companies and individuals that can make unique memorial pieces, such as felted wool figures or stuffed animals in your Ragdoll's likeness.

Though loss is a unique experience for everyone, it's important not to isolate yourself during this time. Isolation will only deepen your sorrow and have a negative effect on your mental health. Instead, try to accept support from others. Your friends and family will be there to support you in your time of need. You may also want to seek out pet loss support groups that may better understand your feelings and offer emotional support. If you are struggling to move beyond your grief, you should seek the guidance of a mental health professional. There are many professionals who specialize in grief counseling and will be able to support you as needed.

Made in the USA
Las Vegas, NV
22 December 2023

83358504R00075